# We All Follow The Cobblers ...Over Land & Sea

A collection of football memories compiled and edited by Mark Kennedy

Text Copyright © Mark Kennedy 2018

Mark Kennedy has asserted rights in accordance with Copyright Designs and Patents Act 1988 to be identified as the author of this work.

All rights reserved

No part of this publication may be lent, resold, hired out or reproduced in any form without written permission of the author and publisher.

First published in 2008 in the UK

Reproduced in 2019

ISBN: 978-1-7391188-1-5
Independently published

## Edition Two

Welcome to edition two of "**WE ALL FOLLOW THE COBBLERS, OVER LAND & SEA**." Originally published in 2008, there have been several requests to get copies since so why not re-release it for all to enjoy?

There have been many changes to football itself since 2008. The rich clubs have got richer, fans pay more to watch their teams, there is more football on television to choose from and expectancy has increased.

Across the country though, many fans still follow their match day rituals and memories and friendships are created.

This book contains the original stories of fans' experiences linked with Northampton Town that were originally published in 2008. There have been a few minor edits but the stories remain the same. Please enjoy these classic nuggets of football memorabilia.

# Introduction

It's only a game! How many times I've heard someone say that! Like many others I've devoted many an hour to this thing that is "only a game." So why do we do it? We spend time, money, effort, get stressed, sing, jump around like loonies, shout, swear, laugh and cry and all this over a game. Well as millions know, it's more than that! Football, is described by some as religion, some say obsession, some say hobby and some simply say because they love it! There is no question about it though; football is the largest sport in the universe!

Like millions of others all over the world, I fell in love with football at an early age. I was born and raised in Northampton, a place that many pass through on the M1, a place that once had a thriving shoe industry within its sleepy boundaries; hence the football team's nickname The Cobblers.

My obsession with the Cobblers started at the age of about four years old, when my mum and I moved to a quiet suburb and our new home happened to be three streets away from the County Ground. I spotted the floodlights towering over the old main stand and became intrigued about football. But my mum had other ideas! She shied away from the violence and trouble at grounds, so used to take me to watch stock car racing instead. I loved our trips to watch the racing, but my interest for the Cobblers lived on even though I didn't attend any games.

A lot of my school friends at my new school, Cedar Road Lower School, started talking football and asked me who I supported, so I told them "Northampton Town." Many of them laughed and told me I should support Liverpool, who were winning everything at the time. The fateful day arrived when Mum bought me my first sports bag for school and guess what it had written on the side? Nope, not Northampton but Tottenham Hotspur. So at school, I became a Tottenham and a Cobblers fan, which wasn't too bad as Ricky Villa had just won the FA Cup with a wonder goal in 1981. My support of Spurs was a schoolboy affair really as I watched for the results on television and the odd live game on 'The Big Match' when I could. But my real love affair and curiosity sat behind the claret gates in Abington Avenue.

My dad, who lives on the south coast, was delighted about my support for Northampton Town, when he visited, he always promised that he'd take me to my first game, as he was a big Cobblers fan too. Fate was never on our side though, every time he ventured to Northampton, we either played away or the game fell victim to the weather.

I finally made my first game at the age of 11 and got hooked like many others have in all four corners of the globe. I'll save the story of my first match until a little later for you. By the way, Dad and I did get to our first game together in 1991 when a penalty from Stuart Bevan five minutes into injury time secured a 2-1 win for the Cobblers. We've been to many others together since.

The Spurs thing faded away in my late school years, I saw no need to pretend I followed a club that I never went to watch. I was now 100% Cobblers. Over the years, I have followed the Cobblers home and away and have made many friends through the club as well as fans of other clubs. In 2002, I was extremely lucky to meet my wife Jules, who is quite keen on football herself and is now a regular in the Cobblers crowd too. We are pictured above in the away end at Kenilworth Road, Luton in 2007.

**Mark Kennedy**

# Chapter 1 - The Good Old Days

*"The miracle of 1966 wasn't England winning the World Cup; it was Northampton playing in the First Division!"* - Joe Mercer.

If you were born before 1966, one would imagine that 1966 would have been an amazing year as far as football was concerned. Fans crammed onto the terraces, no segregation, turn up and pay on the day. No sponsors on the shirts and no grass on the pitch in the winter months.

The following collection of stories really makes you really appreciate what football should be all about. You couldn't jump on a supporters' bus to get to an away game, sometimes an all-day journey would be required to watch your team. One of my good friends Roger Averill will tell you the tale. Roger in fact owns a Cobblers programme from every single game dating back to the Division One season. That's what a loft extension should be for!

Some of the well-worn pictures were sent in by Club Historian Frank Grande. Frank's in-depth knowledge of Northampton Town was second to none. The picture of the helicopter hovering over the pitch was used as part of an army recruitment campaign in the late 60's/early 70's. Frank pointed out that around twenty years later, then Chairman Derek Banks was rebuked a helicopter landing on the County Ground pitch as it could endanger the fans. Nowadays we would barely be allowed a fly by.

Many of you will recognise Dave Bowen standing on the duckboards on the Cricket Side and wandering up the steps of the Spion Kop. The man behind the meteoric rise to the promised land.

Top left, sent in by Glen Cousner, is the original Chronicle & Echo reporting the Cobblers clinching promotion and bottom right shows the players celebrating in the old main stand. Funnily enough, despite top flight football, Northampton still had empty spaces on the terraces on match days.

So read on and picture those memories, squashed on a packed terrace on a cold Saturday afternoon, standing on tip-toe to see above those in front. Imagine the smoke billowing from the chimneys from the neighbouring terraced houses in the tight streets around the area of Abington in Northampton.

## Kingsthorpe Grove Junior School Football Team 1948/49

Anyone who has ever had anything to do with the Cobblers or the County Cricket will have heard of Fanny Walden one of Northamptonshire's famous sons. To refresh the memories Fanny (Frederick Ingram) Walden was born 1st March 1888 in Wellingborough. He played for the Cobblers until transferring to Spurs in April 1913 and, except for an enforced break during World War 1, remained there until July 1924 when he returned to the Cobblers. He played for Spurs 227 times and England twice, it would have been many more but when he was at his peak all football was suspended. His first cap was in 1914 against Scotland and his second against Wales in 1922. He was at 5ft. 2ins. the smallest player to have played for England.

He was also a tremendous cricketer, playing for Northamptonshire from 1910 until 1929 scoring 7538 runs and taking 119 wickets in 258 matches. He then went on umpire in 212 first class matches and 11 test matches from 1930 until 1939. He died in Northampton in May 1949.

**Dainty physique**

His nickname of Fanny was a nickname in common use in the early part of the century to describe anybody of 'dainty physique'. The lad on the far right of the second row was his Grandson, we all called him Fanny. I can never remember him being called by his proper name, not even by Mr

Piggott the headmaster standing next to him or by the other teacher, Mr Bennett. He was thin and wiry just like his famous granddad, and just like his famous granddad nobody could ever catch him.

The photo is of Kingsthorpe Grove Junior School *'Probables'* and *'Possibles'* Football Teams 1947/48. Unfortunately, I cannot remember any of the other lad's names, but I am seated on the floor far right. I hope this photo brings back memories as we had all lived through six dark years but had survived.

**We all read the 'Green Un' until it fell to pieces**

It is interesting to note the variety of shirts and socks, I think the *'Probables'* had the white shirts with collars and the *'Possibles'* had the shirts with the rounded necks, all the socks and shorts were your own as clothes were still on ration at the time. The picture was taken in the playground at the back of the school. We were all Cobblers mad and even if we couldn't afford to go to the games, 6d was a lot of money then - we all read the 'Green Un' in the playground on Monday until it fell to pieces.

**George Phipps (One of the Old Codgers from Coventry)**

## Gunning for Glory

Saturday 27th January 1951 was a significant day in Northampton Town's history as the Cobblers played in front of a crowd of 72,408. The venue was Highbury and the opposition were, of course, Arsenal, in the FA Cup fourth round. Cobblers fan Tony Lyon remembers the day;

"Dad and Mum always stood on the Spion Kop for all the Cobblers home games but the day of the Arsenal game Dad had to work so Mum and I went along. We travelled to North London by train and tube. We joined a long queue outside the ground before this old fella comes along and said to a few of us "Why don't you go around the corner and for four shillings you can sit in the double decker stand?" It was brilliant and there was no queue. The game was a cracker, Jack English he scored both our goals in a 3-2 defeat. Ted Duckhouse was injured and played on the left-wing limping most of the game, we gave a good account of ourselves. That day, we played in blue and Arsenal played in white.

## What's it like to see a crowd

To date, the attendance of 72,408 at Highbury remains the biggest ever to watch a Cobblers fixture. The second biggest was the 1998 Play Off Final v Grimsby which attracted 62,998 and third was 56,939 for the FA Cup Fourth Round Tie at Anfield when the Cobblers lost 3-1 to Liverpool. The biggest ever league crowd to witness Town was just across the road at Goodison when 48,489 saw the opening game of the Division One campaign when Northampton went down 5-2.

It would be hard in this day and age, to imagine a top side pulling in such a big crowd against a team from the bottom tier. The Cobblers were struggling in the league and ended up finishing 21st in Division Three South. Despite this, crowds at the County Ground were in the five figures for most of the season.

**Story inspired by Tony Lyon**

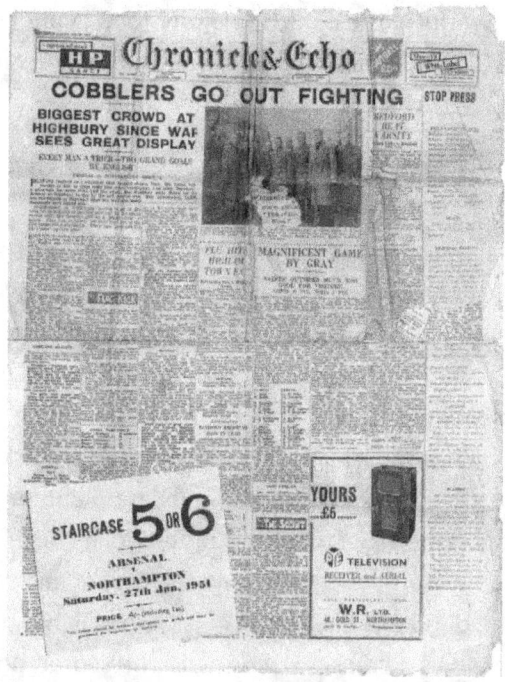

Thanks to Glen Cousner for sending in the original Chronicle and Echo from 27th January 1951 reports the Cobblers' cup tie at Highbury. Also included in the image is Tony's original ticket from the day.

# Humiliation - Circa 1955

I was eight, star-struck, tongue-tied. They were standing there, in our kitchen, actually standing in our kitchen, two Cobblers players, in their tracksuits. Five days before I had watched them at The County Ground and now they were standing there, in our kitchen.

**Starstruck**

Ron Patterson, a tough, cultured left back, and hard-working half back Gwyn Hughes had been persuaded by my dad to come over to Brixworth to take some early-season training sessions with the village team. They came on a number of occasions and after a while my blushing had receded to the claret of the home strip and I was just about able to gulp "Hello" through dry lips that slapped with the effort.

**The pitch was our personal Wembley**

Our games lessons at Brixworth Primary School took place on Farmer Mallard's field behind the church. The pitch, our personal Wembley, showed some signs of having been laid many years before by those great groundsmen Ridge and Furrow and the markings did not conform to league specifications, due to the many incorrectly placed penalty spots and dotted areas deposited by the field's usual occupants, now herded to an adjacent pasture.

One afternoon, Mr Ward-Hopkins, the headmaster, announced we were having a special person to help with our football and into the classroom walked none other than Ron Patterson. Ron gave me a nod of recognition and I felt very proud.

"He's been in our kitchen," I boasted.

"So have I," came the unimpressed reply from Norman Clarke. We put on our wooden-studded boots and clattered out of school and along the path through the churchyard.

Ron set us off on a passing exercise, in threes, up and down the field. Unfortunately, I was on the left of our three and my left foot had a life of its own. We had just got level with Ron when the ball was transferred to me. All I had to do was to knock it to Titch Manning on the right of our trio. I pictured the superbly weighted and directed pass and Ron's smile of delight at my silky skills.

**I landed in a cowpat in front of professional footballer**
How the ball came to deflect off the toe of my supposedly non-kicking right foot I do not know. What I do know is that my left foot swung, made contact with fresh air rather than leather and continued its path with such force that I landed in an ungainly heap and recent cowpat directly in front of a professional footballer.

There was general hilarity from my mates but I was so glad the other members of my footballing family were not there to witness it. I certainly wasn't going to tell them. The story got home before I did. As I entered the house, Mum asked for my smelly kit to wash. Then the version that had been passed to her was recounted to my dad, and embellished in the telling to my many brothers and sister. In the playground the next morning, some lads thought it highly amusing to recreate endless action replays for me long before the technique was popularised by television.

**Ron Cow-Patterson is coming tonight**
But worst of all, Ron and Gwyn (who I was sure knew about my shame) continued to come to our house for a cup of tea before training sessions commenced. Dad found different ways of goading me. "I hope Ron does that passing in threes again - always goes down well, that one" or "Ron Cowpatterson's coming tonight" or "Ron Spatteredon will be here soon." Needless to say, when the Cobblers players arrived, I was always elsewhere. Vivid memories of the incident have been revisited over the intervening years, whenever family footballing prowess was discussed. My advice to anyone over-excited at the prospect of playing in front of a sporting hero is to keep your feet on the ground.

Dave Blake

---

## Attendance 13,325 (and that's just for the reserves)

The most memorable match I saw played at the County Ground was between Northampton and Arsenal on January 4 1958; this was the Third Round of the FA Cup. I was nearly ten years old and had already supported the Cobblers since my eighth birthday. The build-up to this match had begun a month earlier on 7th December 1957 when the Cobblers beat

Bournemouth 4-1 in the FA Cup Second Round. On the following Monday the Cup draw was made and Cup fever began in Northampton and in my household.

**Five shillings a ticket**

A 21,344 maximum was put on the gate, with normal match prices applying; 5,000 tickets were given to Arsenal. The Cobblers were only attracting league attendances of around 7,000 at this time. Tickets for the Cup match were sold at the turnstiles at the next Cobblers reserves home match, which surprisingly was also against Arsenal the following Saturday. A gate of 13,325 turned up for that reserve match to see the Cobblers win 2-1. I secured my ticket for the Main Stand, it only cost five shillings. The Monday prior to the big game the Cobblers team went to Woburn for some light relaxation and golf, and they then resumed normal training but additionally built themselves up with the A Cup elixir of sherry, eggs, glucose and orange juice. On the Wednesday Alan Woan, who the Cobblers had signed from Norwich, went down with food poisoning, and Bobby Tebbutt stood by to take his place.

**Sell all your tickets, you couldn't sell all your tickets**

Arsenal returned 1,500 tickets on the Thursday and another big queue for tickets at the County Ground started to snap them up. On the big day, Arsenal played in gold and the Cobblers played in blue to avoid a clash of colours; Dave Bowen played at left half, and Cliff Holton at right half for the Gunners. Dave Bowen was an Arsenal player, but normally he trained with the Cobblers, but the week before this match he was banned from the County Ground as match day got close.

**Giant killers**

Cobblers kicked off at 2.15pm toward the Hotel End in front of 21,344 excited fans. Tebbutt scored from a Yeoman free kick, which Bowen desperately tried to keep out of the net, but failed. A photo of Bowen's desperate and failed lunge was subsequently circulated into all the sports pages. Arsenal equalised through Clapton, and then Herd hit a post before Hawkins hooked the ball over his shoulder for 2-1 with an hour gone. Leek got the third as a Hawkings cross was cleared into his path with fourteen minutes remaining. The final result - Cobblers 3 Arsenal 1. Gate receipts were £2,700 for the cup match plus the gate receipts from the reserve match and with the fourth round still to come this could be a fruitful cup run for the Cobblers.

Was there ever a bigger crowd for a Cobblers Reserve team match? Was there ever a home FA Cup tie as exciting? I don't think so!

The squads, no subs in those days:

Cobblers: Elvy, Collins, Patterson, Yeoman, Gale, Mills, English, Tebbutt, Hawkings, Leek, Fowler

Arsenal: Kelsey, Wills, Evans, Holton, Dodgin, Bowen, Clapton, Herd, Groves, Bloomfield, Nutt

**Derrick Thompson**

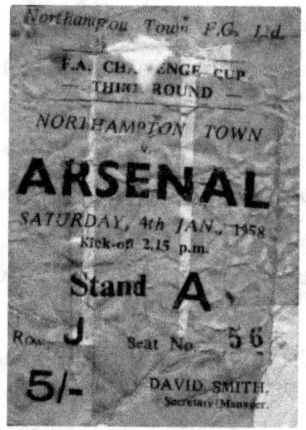

*A well-aged, Derrick's original ticket from that famous giant killing day. Town were beaten 3-1 by Liverpool in Round Four in front of 56,939.*

## Like Rabbits Caught in the Glare of Floodlights

It's an unenviable position to be in, playing against the club that you have supported all of your life. You know that you could beat them, undermining their quest for success, and perhaps even causing the manager to lose his job. True, the Northamptonshire County Youth Cup may have not been The Cobblers' main target for the 1963/4 season but when Cobblers Youth (Under 18's) were drawn in the semi-final against Brixworth Youth (Under 17's), it seemed very important to us in the village team, especially as the game was to be contested under the County

Ground's floodlights. We were to live the dream of playing on the hallowed turf that had been caressed by the passes of our heroes (and, less impressively, parked on by hundreds of cricket fans).

**The problem with the floodlights - they stayed on**

The build-up to the game did not go smoothly, three of our best players deciding to maintain their footballing credibility by not appearing in the game, each citing a pre-booked bout of diarrhoea. They feared we would be humiliated. Personally, I don't feel 14-0 was in any way a humiliation. Firstly, there was a problem with the floodlights. They stayed on. Secondly, there were problems with future first-teamers Ronnie Walton and Ray Perryman, with Bob Frost, Malc Howe, Alan Inwood and the other twenty or so Cobblers youth-teamers who seemed to be playing against us. To this day, I'm not even sure if Roger Barron came back into goal after half-time.

**Our keeper had a comb stored in his socks**

I remember there were a few problems in persuading our third-choice goalkeeper to play and then during the match to stop him using the comb he had stored down one of his socks. I wonder if "Flan" Kennedy later bored his son Mark with edited highlights from his heroic back-bending in front of almost 500 spectators. It has to be said though that, as a keeper, he'd got neat hair.

I was centre half and can only actually remember touching the ball once, making a sliding tackle on Walton to prevent what would have been the all-important fifteenth goal. The crowd rose as one man and by then I think it was. My efforts to stem the tide of attacks led to one of The Cobblers saying, "He's playing like a Canute." At least, that's what I heard. Still, there were some positives. Our centre forward Dave West was so impressive taking fifteen kick-offs that he was later to play for Cobblers Colts. Charlie Barham's statuesque performance at full back was sufficient to gain him a Cobblers' directorship about twenty years later and I did hear some money changed hands in the deal.

It was an experience I wouldn't have missed; to be in the dressing room, to run out of the tunnel, to play under lights in front of spectators who had actually paid to be in the County Ground, even if they regretted it!

**David Blake**

## A Supporter of the Sixties

There were not many cars about in the early 1960's compared to today. The best and easiest way to get to a game at the County Ground was to catch one of the fleet of red buses that used to leave Abington Street almost in convey. By the time they reached the entrance to Abington Park they were almost empty.

If you did not mind the elements and you could not afford the covered or seating area at the Abington Avenue end then the best vantage position was from the duckboards on the cricket side. Entering the Ground from the Wantage Road end it then meant a long walk to the transfer passing through the turnstiles half way along the walk.

Anyone buying a programme as they entered the ground could boast that they had read it by the time they reached their destination. Just an editorial about the last game, a small bit about the reserves and today's opponents, the clubs lists of goal scorers plus of course the line-ups of the day. The rest was made up of adverts. So different from the glossy edition produced today.

*The hallowed car park! The County Ground pictured some years later during the summer months (Pete Norton)*

**It was like a domino effect**
There was some kind of pecking order on the duckboards; children and old men sat on the front and the tallest stood at the back. In between supporters were tightly packed. This sometimes meant that as a child you would sometimes have to watch the game through a haze of pipe smoke coming from the senior citizen sitting next to them. However, that was all accepted in those days. The smell of stale cigarette smoke and Bovril was part and parcel of the game. This must have produced some comical scenes for the rest of the ground when a goal was scored and some supporters would jump up, miss their footing knocking over the person standing next to them when they tried to regain their balance. This caused a 'domino effect', as several people then found themselves fighting to regain their footing. Bob Price the Chronicle and Echo photographer used to take pictures of sections of the crowd, the following Saturday they would appear in the 'green/pink un' with one supporter circled and offered a prize. As soon as it became obvious, supporters would jostle for positions to get into the photograph.

Pre match entertainment was military music played on old 78 records and often the needle stuck without anyone in authority noticing for some time. As well as the programme also on sale were raffle tickets, first prize was the match ball although a cash award of £5 later replaced this! No announcements in those days so when the draw was made a ball boy would parade twice round the ground with the winning numbers chalked on a blackboard. This used to provide some entertainment when it rained! It would be impossible not to mention the 'man on a ladder'. In the programme were a list of 'other games' relating to the division the Cobblers were in. Each game had a letter by it. These letters related to a board situated near the bowls club end of the ground and just before the end of the game a man would gingerly climb a ladder and hang numbers by each letter which would be the half time score of the corresponding game. No sooner had he put them up than he took them down again!

**Twenty minutes of free football**
The club used to open the gates around twenty minutes before the end of the game allowing youngsters who could not afford to watch the game to watch the closing stages. It also allowed others in and it was not

unusual as a game wound down to a tense finish to hear the cry: 'Chronicle!' This was generally met with loud jeers.

You were also close to the players and often heard the comments made by the players. Tommy Fowler once left a full back standing for the umpteenth time during a match. In a desperate attempt the frustrated player tried a slide tackle but missed his target as Tommy showed him a pair of clean heels. His frustration boiled over when he called out after, "Tommy you bugger."

Theo Foley took the ball off a winger who was later to be a 'name' in the football world. He tackled the player and cleared the ball.

'Who do you think you are?' The frustrated player asked still sitting on the floor. 'Theo Foley, captain of Northampton Town and Ireland!' That said it all.

**Frank Grande (Club Historian)**

*Fans sit feet from the touch line to watch the Cobblers v Fulham in 1966. This was the last time that First Division Football would be viewed from the infamous duck boards. Fulham won the match 4-2 to condemn the Cobblers to relegation. Notice how close to the touch line some of the younger fans at the front are! Could you imagine that in the Premiership today? (Pete Norton)*

# Early Press Days

A top hospital administrator named Stanley Hill had been doing commentary on the Cobblers for many years through the fifties and sixties (and possibly earlier) along old-fashioned landlines which went from a point at the County Ground to Northampton General, Manfield, and Creaton hospitals (only the General still exists). The signal was then routed via big glowing valve amplifiers through the hospital wired systems and into the ancient bakelite headsets that were at each bedside.

*The legendary Dave Bowen on the Spion Kop (Frank Grande)*

## A beetroot-headed Bowen retreated back to his office

In the early seventies, I was involved in the formation of Radio Nene Valley along with a committee of ten others, all with the backing of Stanley Hill, and we formed a music and speech radio station with a studio based in what used to be a nurse's bedroom on the top floor along Billing Road in Northampton. Stanley's Cobblers' commentaries continued, and we put the other programmes around them.

As it happened, we'd assembled a talented group of presenters, and as I was not at all happy with the quality of the match day announcers at the County Ground, I ventured in one day to the offices under the main stand and made a suggestion to the great Dave Bowen, who I think at that stage was General Manager, that we could do a good job for them through the match day microphones at the ground, and it wouldn't cost them a dime. Well, you'd think I'd said something worthy of treason. He went absolutely livid, screaming and shouting in his distinctive Welsh voice while I tried to stay calm and explain how good it would be for the club. In the end, with him at top volume of "How dare you, what the bloody hell do you know?" I retreated backwards out of the door onto Abington Avenue, telling him we really could do better for the spectators. He pursued me in a totally unintelligible rant until we were outside an electrical shop that many readers will remember as Bruce Bunker's. At this point the now beetroot-headed Bowen turned and stalked back to his office, shouting obscenities at me all the way. I was totally staggered by the experience and at the time my hero worship went downhill a bit!

Graham Carr was another of our great managers and when BBC Northampton asked me to cover a game at Lincoln in the eighties, I was excited to know that I'd be able to get his opinions on tape after the game. Everything went wrong, during the game we couldn't properly hear talkback from the studio in our headphones, but blundered on, at least I felt happy that I'd be able to get Graham's words of wisdom after the game. Well, the job of a sports reporter is rarely glamorous, and this was the pits as we had lost badly. On top of this Carr was so angry and upset he had a long session with the lads in the dressing-room and then failed to come and meet the Press. I could not come back with a blank tape, so sent in some appeals and he eventually appeared from the bar area at nearly seven o'clock. He wasn't unpleasant with me but he really didn't want to speak and to make things worse he kept turning away from the microphone as he spoke. When I eventually got back to BBC Northampton, I just managed to edit enough material together for Sunday Sport to make a fist of it!

Before we had any local radio for Northampton it was my job and that of a colleague called Dick Gee to manhandle our heavy Uher "portable" tape recorders to the County Ground to get the then-manager Bill Dodgin Jnr's comments for our sports service on Radio Nene Valley for the hospital patients. Bill was a character and knew football inside-out. It was largely due to his work that local boy Phil Neal was brought to the attention of Liverpool and then of course he went on to captain England.

When us hacks entered Bill's little office under the main stand after each home game, he was not in the habit of giving a quick quote and then kicking us out. He'd say nothing at all about the football until he'd uncorked a bottle of Scotch, took out his collection of glasses, and handed them round. Then, after the drinking session he'd always give Dick and me pride of place with the first questions, even if the national press was present. He'd give us loads of stuff that was "off the record" including his cutting views of the directors of the club. He was one of the last truly gentleman managers, which is why I was saddened to hear recently from a friend that in his later years he wandered his - I think Hampshire - village in the throes of dementia, but was always treated well by the community who knew him to have been such a lovely man.

One other memory was the game when we'd gone up to Roker Park in the early 60s to meet the newly-relegated Sunderland, while we, the new boys to Division 2, were expected to get pulled to pieces.

Joe Kiernan captained the side, Theo Foley headed a cannon of a shot off the line and nearly went into the net himself, and we did the impossible and won 2-0 while my brother and I jumped up and down like maniacs, this before the days of segregation and not a single Sunderland supporter laid a hand on us. They were completely stunned.

We stayed in the area with our parents and on the Monday my aunt, who was billeted in Newcastle with the Salvation Army, arranged for us to go down an old-type drift-mine. We walked down there, eventually getting deep underground and seeing all the pit ponies. At one narrow seam of coal we watched the men working in impossibly cramped and filthy conditions, cutting swathes of coal with seeming ease using hand-held cutters. One man called me forward and asked me to try, I couldn't even lift the damn thing.

Well, the point of the story is, that man turned out to be the brother of Billy Hails, who had played on the right wing for the Cobblers in our famous victory just two days earlier! How times have changed!

**Steve Riches**

# Funny Things Happened to Me on the Way to the Match

It was late April 1966, England had yet to win the World Cup, but the Cobblers were in the First Division. It was Saturday and we were playing Fulham who were struggling, like us, at the wrong end of the table. We had to win and a big crowd was expected at the County Ground.

**A bunch of bar stewards**

Me, Dave, Jimmy and Danny were bar stewards at the Monkey House (Monks Park WMC), part time of course. Dave and I also worked for a car firm full time, Jimmy and Danny were drinkers full time and sometimes got some overtime in. We decided earlier in the week that we were all going to the match, but definitely had to get a few drinks in beforehand to help ease the tension.

Me and Dave had to work a few hours on Saturday morning, but met the other two after in the Bull & Butcher down Bridge Street. They did great cheese rolls in there. So there we were, drinks all round. Afterwards we had to do the Bell and then Saddlers before poshing it up with a rum and blackcurrant in the Dolphin Bar in the Grand Hotel on Gold Street. Then it was bottled beer only in the Shipmans before the Queens and the Palmerston on the market square. We seemed to miss out the Rifle Drum for some reason, but we were happy and hungry, so someone suggested some nice greasy food.

**It all started to go wrong**

We bumped into a bloke we knew in Abington Street and said we were on our way to the big match, he said he would come along too. This was the point when it all started to go horribly wrong!

Swanny was a bus conductor who liked to drink a few and a few was all it took. Time was moving on so we moved swiftly to the Mermaid Café in Fish Street. This was also a bad choice! The five of us ordered the egg, beans and chips option in the downstairs area. When the food arrived, we began to wonder why we felt hungry at all, but Swanny tucked into his food, boasting a 'gut of iron'. Unfortunately, the foundry in his stomach was chucking out that time and he heaved all of his Mermaid Special all over the floor. The waitress rushed upstairs to tell her boss and being the true mates that we were, we quickly moved to another table as far away as possible. The boss arrived with a mop and bucket demanding we cleaned the mess up, but only found Swanny slumped over the table. We denied knowing him and said we didn't feel well either, blaming the cooking for our illness. The waitress dobbed us in though, saying that we all came in together. The boss then started getting nasty so we ran leaving Swanny to mop up his brunch. We didn't know him that well.

**How could we miss the golden mile?**
Time was still ticking away and we were at the wrong end of the Welly Road, but how could we miss out on the pubs along Northampton's Golden Mile. The Cobblers needed us but so did the brewery and we were all beginning to realise that all the fluid that had gone in had to come out. We arrived in the Racehorse about two o clock to use the facilities. Whilst me and Dave went to the gents, Jimmy and Danny bought more beer. Well I did tell you they were professionals! Me and Dave were about boozed up and were ready to go to the football by now but we managed to politely squeeze down a few mouthfuls. Then it was full speed ahead to the County Ground in time for kick off. We now must have looked more like a bunch of drunks at 2.30am not 2.30pm.

We managed to avoid the Monkey House on the way but Danny had to pee in an alleyway, returning with splashes all over the legs of his smart suit and highly polished black brogues. Very funny! We arrived at the Spion Kop end at a quarter to three, the atmosphere outside was great. We had the great crowd just like we wanted. That afternoon 24,523 watched the Cobblers lose to Fulham but we didn't because it was a lock out. The ground was full! At this moment Swanny appeared at the end of Abington Avenue

Of course, the crowd on this day still remains the record attendance for a Cobblers home fixture, we were always sure that they could have fitted another three of us in there somewhere.

The names have been changed to avoid being sued for defamation.

**Patrick Kennedy**

# Trial and Error

**A chance to live the dream**

The great day approached - 18th November 1967. Soon I would be taking up my rightful position in the ranks of Northampton Town's professional footballers. Almost certainly reaching the higher echelons and becoming part of the club's folklore, assuming Godlike status throughout the county, and probably country, as international honours could not be ruled out. But first I had to play in the Sunday morning practice match at the County Ground and convince the powers to be, of my football genius. A mere formality, obviously.

For mere, read mare as in nightmare for that's how it turned out. What should have been my launch pad into an exciting new career became a damp squib, nose diving into obscurity. And it was my own entire fault. I played for my local side, Irthlingborough Rangers and they contacted the Cobblers regarding my enormous... er, talent. The trial was arranged for that fateful Sunday.

**Party on dudes**

Unfortunately, a house party had been arranged for the Saturday night and I had been invited. Now a responsible person with a sound mind with the chance to play for the club that he has supported all his life, would have little difficulty in declining this offer, wouldn't he? Well no he wouldn't, actually, he'd have a lot of difficulty. "Of course, I'll be there" I said stupidly. Well I was young and impetuous and had also discovered girls, apparently, they had been there all the time but I hadn't noticed. So the lure of the opposite sex and the party overcame the lure of an alcohol-free early night in preparation for my big match.

After returning home in the early hours of Sunday morning from the said party, I managed to sleep a little and arrived at The County Ground for the ten o'clock kick off in a state of neither physical or mental fitness. Obviously if I'd have played in my regular midfield position, I would have been another Richard Hill. In fact, I would have been Richard Hill before Richard Hill was Richard Hill. As it was Roly Mills threw me a shirt and said "You're playing full back son."

**Foreigners in football back then**
At first, I thought the other trialists were speaking in a foreign language until I realised, they were Geordies. We played for about half an hour then most players were replaced by others. I remember thinking "Great, I could do with a rest" as the lad I was marking would surely go on to play for England. But for some strange reason I had to stay on and mark another winger with the athletic prowess of *Linford Christie*. I mean, come on, this was the before the invention of substitutes and totally unfair. So I spent the rest of the game in pursuit of the footballing equivalent of *Roadrunner*. I was a creative midfielder for Christ's sake, I wasn't supposed to charge up and down the field like a headless chicken.

**Pretty patterns**
Back then football was less physically orientated. When inside forwards still existed and wingers... worse luck. Before things got sophisticated and complicated and skill got suffocated with various systems and patterns. When Terry Venables' Christmas Tree formation was still a twinkle in Trafalgar Square.

What could I do then? Here was a skillful Geordie lad, far more talented than I was, possibly taking his first steps to stardom. To give him a helping hand or foot, to a few more steps - the concrete steps of the Cobblers terracing - would be unthinkable! How can anything be unthinkable when you have already thought it, is beyond me. So I decided that I wouldn't think it, I would just do it.

**Fifty ways to leave your full back**
Well he had it coming, didn't he? Travelling 250 miles to humiliate me. And I don't expect that he'd been to a party the night before either, he'd probably been tucked up in bed by ten o'clock with a good book "Stanley Matthews - Fifty Ways to Make Your Full Back Look A Complete Tw*t." And anyway, all Geordies call women 'pet'. Now a pet to me is something you keep in a cage and stroke occasionally, or take for a walk. So obviously women's emancipation never reached Newcastle.

It was now becoming clear. I would be striking a massive blow for oppressed women throughout the world by kicking this... this... Geordie chauvinist as far back to Newcastle as possible, that I was convinced of. I had become Emily Pankhurst in a Cobblers strip.

**Beep Beep**

Alas my devilish plan to remove *Roadrunner* from the proceedings in one foul swoop, or crude tackle failed miserably. This was a combination of exhaustion and physic powers. My exhaustion and his physic powers, he could see it coming from a mile away. The only difference between my efforts and *Wiley Coyote's* was that I didn't disappear over a 500-foot cliff in the process.

**Wheatley is a ...**

At least I can say that I played at the County Ground. It may have only been a practice match and devoid of any atmosphere, but I don't care. I also avoided any possibility of the Hotel End chanting "Wheatley is a w*nker." Actually, that has quite a worrying ring to it.

My dad, who had been watching the whole debacle from the stand said "Never mind, you did your best."

But did I? I was ill prepared for the game and who knows what may have happened in different circumstances? But of course, then I would have no excuse to fall back on at all. I honestly think that I was never good enough to make it as a professional footballer, although lack of talent hasn't stopped some people from becoming that.

I received the obligatory thanks, but no thanks letter a few days later. Then it eventually sank in that I would be spending my future days on the County Ground terracing not the turf.

**Nigel Wheatley**

*The famous Hotel End, not quite full to capacity to watch the great trial in 1967 (Lee Wade)*

# Kinnell - A Cobblers Legend

I was pleased when Mark asked me to contribute to this, his latest publication. We met, some years ago, as adjacent seat season ticket holders in the West Stand and I soon realised that, like fellow contributor Dave Blake, I had been at school with Mark's dad! This, of course, makes me feel quite old! It has not been easy, though, to sift through forty odd years of memories of supporting the Town, through thin and thin! Here, though, are just a few snippets and thoughts!

**I had never kicked a ball that wasn't egg shaped**
It was reaching the First Division in the mid-sixties that started it all off for me. Until then I had never kicked a ball that wasn't egg-shaped but when I started playing footie for my office team in 1965. I soon realised firstly, what a hard game it was and, secondly how utterly useless I was at it!
I was sponsored by Subbuteo and spent most of my time trying to get back onto my feet. Hence, over the years, this has made me more tolerant of players who, may be, were not having the best of times on the pitch.
Like many others I can recall games at the old County Ground where, standing on the 'Cricket Side' we were 'up close and personal' with the players. Quite disconcerting when you saw someone called *'Killer'* Kurila or Graham Carr hurtling towards you! I often wonder what might have happened if Alan Carr had managed the Cobblers, rather than Graham!
I recall one dismal mid-week night game in the last period of Dave Bowen's managership. It was the time of year very close to bonfire night and we were losing at half-time. There was an eerie silence in the ground and someone let off a banger in the Hotel End. This was followed by a very loud shout from one long suffering supporter, "Bowen's shot hisself!"
The legendary Fulham game at the County Ground in many ways typifies the luck of the team. Sitting comfortably in the lead at half time with well over 20,000 people in the ground, we appeared to be staying in the top flight at Fulham's expense! The rest, of course, is history. Yet Fulham, in more recent years saw themselves matched against the Cobblers in the lower divisions. In the year when Kevin Keegan bought Paul Peschisolido for the club for a large fee, I remember in embarrassment hearing my

wife, then a season ticket holder, joining in the chanting with the rest of the Cobblers fans 'What a waste of money!'

**We were lucky to get nil**

When I was younger the one thing I always dreaded was Monday mornings at work. Especially after a 5-0 defeat where, as Tommy Docherty used to say 'we were lucky to get the nil!' Everyone else seemed to support teams that never lost a match. It seemed that my colleagues couldn't wait to enjoy themselves at the expense of this sad Cobblers supporter. Why I tried defending the indefensible I will never knew it was just hopeless.

Even though I don't work Mondays any more, I still have Saturday evenings to cope with. My wife, now supporting via Radio Northampton, anticipates my mood based on the match commentary. Of late I have tended to change my approach to Saturdays by rehearsing the inevitable and making all the excuses before I leave for Sixfields. 'We hit the woodwork six times, the ref didn't give us a thing all day and they had one shot at goal in ninety minutes and it went in off a stray dog that had run onto the pitch!

**Pelted with sandwiches**

Over the years I have visited a number of really awful grounds following the Town. I recall Bristol Rovers in the first leg of the play offs when my wife and I were standing just below a section of the ground reserved for Bristol's wheelchair supporters. It was bizarre! Throughout the game they pelted us all with sandwiches and sausage rolls and one chap even poked my wife on the head with his walking stick! Of course, none of us able-bodied people had the nerve to sort them out. Nor did the police who watched it all happening. We did, though of course, thoroughly enjoy the return match at Sixfields.

The Manchester United FA Cup game in 2004 was interesting – not so much for the match, but for my marathon eight-hour ticket queuing heroics which, after midnight, almost got me reported to the police as a missing person!

There is a bit of a theory that some of us Town supporters are very hard to please – we want to win all games 5-0 and tend to pick on certain of our own players and give them a hard time. Bearing in mind our dismal gates of 5,000, it seems also that many folk are apathetic towards the plight of the club.

Over my long years as a supporter I have thought long and hard for solutions to these problems, but in the end, I guess I just couldn't be bothered!

But back to the question posed earlier – Kinnell – a Cobblers legend? Over my forty or so years this man seems to have been ever-present on the pitch! How can this be so? Take it from me, during all this time I have heard some of our supporters moaning on and on and on:

'Kinnell – what's he doing now?'

'Kinnell – How did he miss that?'

'Kinnell – I'm not coming here anymore!!'

But, of course, like me, they always do come back for more!

**Mike Hermann**

*Was it worth queuing for eight hours? After being almost reported as a missing person by his wife Su, he didn't have to rely on the Sky cameras which captured Manchester United's 3-0 win at Sixfields on their way to an FA Cup Final victory over Millwall. You can guarantee that he saw Kinnell playing for the Cobblers that day too! (Pete Norton)*

# Hooliganism

**How many men went home with the wrong caps?**

Having gone to my first Cobblers game in 1972, I was devastated that I missed the 'good old days' where everyone stood together on the terracing shoulder to shoulder with supporters of the opposition armed with nothing more than a suit, a tie, a flat cap and the occasional rattle. The standard goal celebration no matter how crucial was to throw your cap in the air. How many men must have gone back to their wives at night with the wrong caps, or worse still, none at all.

Although there was a very small element of trouble in those days, it all seemed to escalate in my first few years of watching the Town. With the flared trouser, knitted jumper, scarves around the wrist and toilet roll throwing brigade emulating the clubs with the most notorious hooligan element of the day, most football matches, especially away, were transformed from a quiet day out to one of a frightening experience. Apart from hidden scarves, no one wore club shirts, so most of the time everyone was inconspicuous. Doc Martens, skinheads and crombies were a slight give away but you didn't know whose side they were all on. Running battles were often common up and down Abington Avenue, it was ideal for troublemakers because the area had quite a few alleyways. The Spion Kop was the end of the County Ground which housed away fans, and being an uncovered terrace bought constant amusement to Cobblers fans in the relative comfort of a covered end. It was rather open to the elements, both wind and sun, sometimes the crowd's attention would turn away from the action on the pitch to watch any ensuing scuffles which seemed to break out on a regular basis.

**In those days there was no CCTV**

In fact, it was 'allegedly' a small gang of so-called Cobblers fans who week in, week out infiltrated their way onto the terracing, slowly moved their way into the centre before erupting in a big melee, only to be moved on by the police. Of course, in those days, CCTV cameras did not exist, nor banning orders, so the perpetrators were free to return week after week. Portsmouth in 1979 stands out in my mind. I believe it was the last game of the season and Pompey had just clinched promotion and their fans turned up in their thousands. The Spion Kop was heaving, the Hotel End was full of blue and white but everyone still talks about the fans that decided to get a better view by climbing to the top of the floodlights. I hasten to add that the small element of Cobblers hooligans was nowhere to be seen that day.

The next decade bought violence at most grounds with battles at Reading, Mansfield, Peterborough and various run ins with Swindon were only surpassed by an afternoon out in Chesterfield. Earlier that season, several Spireites hooligans thought they could "take" the Hotel End, and soon after word got around that a revenge trip to Derbyshire was on the cards. The whole world and its mother seemed to turn up that day. There were punters from Northampton in all four sides of the ground clearly looking for trouble, at around 3pm all hell was let loose as the Northampton hooligans took their end. This seemed to spark a huge pitch invasion and no one was going to stand in the way.... even the police to a battering. The next day it was headline news, and despite most people thinking it was a deplorable act, it was accepted as a way of life in those days.

Several bigger, more troublesome games came and went, but by the mid-nineties with the introduction of the cameras, stricter sentences and The Taylor Report, hooliganism seemed to have slowly died down, not completely, because with the invention of the internet, a football ground was not the ideal place to meet to have a punch up, this now happened miles away from anywhere.

There is hardly any ground now where it you wouldn't see hundreds of home and away shirt cladded fans milling around and drinking together as families are coming back to 'the beautiful game'. The threat of razor blades, knuckle dusters, darts and firms like the ICF now seem a thing that only appear in films and to be honest, I'm glad. I can now take my family to any Cobblers games and wear colours with pride, safe in the knowledge that with all the cameras around, a football stadium today is probably the safest place to be.

**Andy Trasler**

# In Praise of the Cricket Side

21st century health and safety officers would have had an absolute field day inspecting the Cricket Side at the County Ground. The flat wooden constructions on which early arrivals stood would not conform to the current Duckboard-Lewis system. The angle of the sloping platforms was ten degrees above permitted elevation and the woodworm per square metre far exceeded present E.U. quotas. Not for the first time, the club had paid money for old rope. This was stretched between poles to provide the only barrier against pitch invasion and the tripping up of linesmen by umbrella handle. In addition, the human rights of ball-boys were breached every time they had to chase a clearance by Colin Gale / Terry Branston / Frank Rankmore / Steve Terry / Sammo (please add central defender of own choice) across the vast acreage of the cricket pitch.

**Close to the hurly burly of the game**

The Cricket Side was a great place from which to watch a match. Facing was the wooden main stand with unyielding, uncomfortable seats; to the right, the steep slope of Spion Kop, usually given over to away fans, where the only shelter was beneath a Tony Ansell's burger; to the left, the terraces, crush barriers and ramshackle roof of the Hotel End, behind which stood the archetypal foul-smelling, pee-highest-up-the wall toilets. The Cricket Side ensured fresh air, on occasions too much of it in the form of back-numbing winter winds from the Wantage Road end. Spectators loved being so close to the action and on this side of the ground you could hear more of what was going on during the hurly-burly of the game, including, surprisingly, the occasional use of rather industrial language, (mainly from visiting players of course). Cricket fans love the thwack of leather on willow; on the Cricket Side you could hear the thwack of John Kurila on opponents.

The crowd scenes on the Cricket Side were aided by the fact that a regular cast trod the boards there. It was a repertory company able to adapt to any drama, any tragedy, any farce. There were comedians, loyal and hardy, morbid and wise, quick-witted ad libbers feeding off the misfortunes of players and the men in black. There were also discontents, les miserables, who used the same script whatever the play. "Lines, stay on the bloody wing" was one oft-repeated refrain. Hundreds though were just happy to stay as members of the chorus. All exited stage left at the end of each performance, whether they had been part of humdrum am-dram or an occasion worthy of a greater stage.

**Bring back the duck boards**

The Cricket Side was certainly a major factor in the County Ground's uniqueness. There have been many pleas for the return of terracing but no "Bring back the duckboards" petitions so it can be assumed such facilities have been consigned to history. However, it must be noted that no duckboards are presently available on eBay. Perhaps this dearth is due to the fact that stocks have already been bought and stored locally, in preparation for a sixties-retro style for the re-development of Sixfields Stadium. The plans are eagerly awaited.

**Dave Blake**

*The Cricket Side in the 1990s, as viewed from the Spion Kop (Tranmere on Tour)*

# The World's Greatest Footballer Comes to Town

Kim Book falls to the ground as George Best rounds him with ease and smashed the ball into the net to score his sixth goal of the afternoon. Many of us Cobblers never thought we would get to see the 'greatest player in the world' as George had just completed a ban for one of his many misdemeanours. It is rumoured that he was still drunk as he leaned on the post to sort of celebrate his sixth goal.

**A modest 3-0 score line**

Almost twenty-four years later, The Cobblers met the might of Manchester United again in the FA Cup and a certain Christano Ronaldo would grace the Northampton turf that day. He played his part in a comfortable, if less spectacular win for the visitors this time around. A couple of scrambled goals and Chris Hargreaves putting through his own net provided a modest 3-0 win instead of the ten-goal spectacle before. It is impossible to compare the two games of course! Different eras and different grounds, the County Ground with George Best playing on what was only a few months earlier was the cricket's car park does not detract from a great spectacle at the old County Ground. The pitch was almost like a ploughed field that day, although a ploughed field would have probably been smoother.

Cobblers fan John Atkinson comments;

"All ticket games didn't happen that often in the good bad old days, Cobblers fans had to attend two games to get vouchers to entitle us to a ticket, as there were no season ticket holders in the seventies. The crowd that day was well below the capacity. Those standing at the very back of the Hotel End would have noticed that there was a huge space. Goal keeper Kim Book had a great game in goal, but the score line does not reflect that in anyway, Best's sheer class was the difference. Of course, Lee Harper had a moment to savour in the 2004 clash, saving Diego Forlan's second minute penalty after Ronaldo was allegedly fouled."

Programmes were also plentiful in the seventies, some being sold in Mr Smith's the local newsagent, this contrasts with the match at Sixfields. Programmes were sold out hours before kick-off, with only around 7000 were printed."

Tickets were like gold dust in 2004 with the club choosing to make a few extra quid on tickets, charging double the normal entry for the visit of one of the world's most famous teams. It was a shame that Alex Ferguson fielded a lower strength side at Sixfields. Notably, Manchester United subsidised their fans ticket prices by paying a tenner towards the cost of entry. Something they didn't have to do as the 1300 seats would have sold no matter what. It is amazing what a club with money can do! Things were similar in 1970 when the club decided to raise admission charges from about 25 pence to around 50 pence (in today's terms).

Christano Ronaldo grabs Martin Smith's shirt during the 2004 NTFC v Manchester United FA Cup tie. (Pete Norton)

**The closest I got that day was shaking hands with him at the end**
Television cameras were in attendance at both games, Sky broadcast the whole thing live in 2004 and showed footage from 1970 in the build-up. The goals from that famous day were captured and have been replayed over and over again. As George scores, he turns and strolls back to the halfway line as cool as you like. There was no sponsor emblazoned across his shirt, but that shirt was reported to have fetched around twenty grand at auction in 2006. Roy Fairfax was quoted to have said that the closest he got to George that day was when he shook hands with him at the end of the match.

The first game put George up there with the legends of soccer with his six-goal burst, it is doubtful that the second game will live as long in the memories of Cobblers fans.

**Inspired by John Atkinson**

*An old grainy picture of George Best at the County Ground in 1970. Notice the packed Cricket Side and the temporary television gantry in the back ground. The camera pointing straight at us captured the famous images that were shown over and over again. (Pete Norton)*

# Chapter 2 - The Yo-yo Years

The previous chapter gave a real down to earth account of the era surrounding the rise and fall from the grace of the First Division glamour, but back then footballers were footballers and not celebrities, like some at the top of today's game. But some things never change, "Kinnell is still a Cobblers legend." Other than Kinnell the Cobblers legend, the main thing that failed to change in Northampton Town's history, was the ability to become a fashionable side. By the 1969/70 season the Cobblers were back in the basement division and things looked pretty depressing. The adventure appeared to be over and there was little to shout about once the roller coaster had seemed to grind to a halt.

But on the 15th November 1969, the safety bars locked into place as a new ride ground into motion. The Cobblers drew 0-0 at home to Weymouth, but it was the beginning of another adventure for County Ground regulars. Eight games and almost three months later one mighty famous day was about to unfold in town and it was all thanks to the magic of the FA Cup. Weymouth were beaten 3-1 in a reply, before Exeter were disposed of at the third attempt in a week. A 1-1 draw was followed by a goalless replay at Exeter and then a second replay which the Cobblers won 2-1. The third round opponents weren't hugely glamorous, but Brentwood were seen off at the first attempt 1-0 to set up a fourth round tie at Tranmere. After a 0-0 draw at Prenton Park, Northampton won the replay 2-1 and set up that famous tie with Manchester United. The next question, would George Best play?

Nobody really felt is necessary to write any more about the seventies in this book, although 1975/76 ended in promotion behind Lincoln City and the Cobblers went the whole season unbeaten at the County Ground. One season later and it was hello to the basement again and that was pretty much it until a Geordie by the name of Graham Carr arrived in town.

**Early Memories**

My earliest memory of actually witnessing the Cobblers play was on a football special in 1983. European Champions Aston Villa won 1-0 at the County Ground and the highlights on a Sunday afternoon. It was the first time I can recall seeing inside the County Ground, all thanks to TV.

A few years later, the facia of the old main stand on Abington Avenue gradually disappearing after the Bradford fire encouraged authorities to make tough safety restrictions on football grounds. Northampton couldn't afford the necessary repairs and a piece of the ground disappeared. From the outside, the temporary 'Meccano Stand' was visible. At first it looked quite impressive from the road, but the building work stopped and we were left with a beloved feature for travelling fans to take the Mickey out of. On a serious note, the Bradford fire shortly followed Hysel more reasons why my mum wasn't keen to let me go.

We always used to wander into the ground after school or in the holidays and have a kick about on the pitch. Nobody ever chucked us out.

This chap Graham Carr started making some shrewd signings and the optimism started to rise. The following season I started to keep my first scrapbook of paper clippings and, with the help of my nan, we built up a little collection. Saturdays consisted of Football Focus on the BBC, flicking straight over the ITV for Saint & Greavsie and then a shopping trip to town before rushing home to catch final score. I used to love the closing headlines, Bruce Hornsby and the Range's *Some Things Never Change* played in the background as the summariser went through the day's events. The football headlines normally finished with, "..and in Division Four, Northampton continue to fly high at the top of the league, today putting x amount past so and so to go x number of points clear..." It was like a dream and I wanted to be part of it.

One of my school mates, Lee Wade, who you will meet in the next few pages, would update me on the match at school on the Monday and I would work out ways to finally get to a match. Everyone at school started to wear claret scarves instead of Liverpool ones now.

The Cobblers were now scoring machines and a Northampton fixture meant goals aplenty. How is this for a run?

(Cobblers scores first): 2-1, 6-3, 4-2, 3-2, 4-2, 3-2, 3-0, 3-3, 1-0, 3-1, 5-0, 4-0, 2-2, 3-1, 4-0, 4-1, 3-2, 1-1, 5-0, 1-0, 1-1 ...and that was just in the league... These 21 matches unbeaten were sandwiched between two defeats to Swansea. The Cobblers went to Halifax, conceded three, but amazingly scored six. In that mini run of five games, the defence shipped eleven goals. It didn't matter though as twenty were scored at the other end. By now, there seemed like no stopping the Cobblers. Crowds were pouring through the turnstiles and everyone was Cobblers mad.

**The big day arrived - my first game**

The crowd went bezerk as the players threw their shirts into the crowd. "Get em off, get em off, get em off...." was the chant from the thousands on the pitch as next followed their shorts. The sight of Richard Hill, Trevor Morley and co standing at the back of the main stand in only their Y-fronts would normally be enough to make a young lad turn the other way in disgust, by this was a glorious night and what a way to celebrate your first game. It was 29th April 1987, Northampton Town v Crewe Alexandra. We were right in the middle of spring and I rushed in from school, threw my uniform off and put on a t-shirt and jeans. There was still almost four hours until kick off, but I was buzzing.

**Fans turned out in their thousands to steal our parking spaces**

As mentioned, for many years my mum wouldn't let me go to the football. There was too much trouble for a kid who hadn't even reached his teens, so I had to make do with watching the crowds sidle past our Abington home. Mum would moan about the parking on match days, as fans grabbed any spots in surrounding streets. This year had been particularly bad, Graham Carr's revolutionary team had won back the fans and they turned in their thousands to *steal* our parking spaces. Finally she gave in! Her friend ray, who was a season ticket holder, agreed to take me to the final game of the season. At 12 years old I was going to see my first live football match and I wouldn't have to listen to the radio, look at Teletext or wait for the Chronicle & Echo or Sports Pink Un, this time I was going to be there. Several phone calls were exchanged between my school mate, Lee Wade and myself as the minutes ticked by. If the Cobblers were to win tonight, we would be certain champions, all bar Preston winning by thirty odd goals in their next few games.

**We shuffled along the street**

Finally, the long-awaited knock at the door sounded and it was Ray, Mum's friend. I wouldn't let him in the house, I wanted to make the short walk to the County Ground. We shuffled along a whole three streets and into Abington Avenue. At the turnstile, it cost a whole pound to get into the Family Enclosure. After walking up a couple of steps and onto the terrace, the view was a picture, thousands of faces packed around the pitch. Directly to the left was a packed Spion Kop, opposite a line of fans on the Cricket Side and beyond the 'Meccano Stand' on my left was the Hotel End in full voice. "Champions, Champions, Champions" was the chant, followed by "Northampton La La La" so I joined in.

I had now found Lee and we made our way to the front to take up our pitch side view. Suddenly there was a massive roar as the Champions to be emerged out of the tunnel. The whole Family Enclosure ran onto the pitch to get autographs, I returned from the bumpy playing area the proud owner of Peter Gleasure's signature. My first autograph.

**Was that a penalty I stupidly asked?**
The match kicked off and I didn't know where to look, did I watch the action, the crowd, sing, shout or chant? I did a bit of everything. I had no idea of how good a game it was but midway through the first half the Cobblers went on the attack and a massive cheer went around the ground as Trevor Morley hit the deck.
"Is that a penalty?" I stupidly asked as everyone went delirious. Dave Gilbert slid the ball home for 1-0, which is how it remained until half time.

**Lee held a hotdog above his head as we celebrated**
Having only eaten a couple of triangles of Toblerone since school dinner, I then became a real Cobblers fan and sampled my first ever hot dog from the purveyors of fine football catering inside the ground. Lee decided on a late hot dog and missed the kick off for the second half, although he could watch from the food hut at the back of the terrace. As he walked back down the terrace, Richard Hill burst through the Crewe defence and fired home a low shot. We were jumping around like loonies; Lee held his hotdog high above his head as we chanted the goal scorer's name over and over again.
The only other part of the match that I could remember was a late long-range consolation goal from Crewe's Peter Bodak that was greeted with a muted cheer from a handful of travelling fans shoved somewhere in a lorry trailer next to the bowling green.
The final whistle went and almost everyone on the terrace was on the pitch to celebrate the new champions. This was a perfect start to my experience as a Cobblers fan and I've been hooked ever since. Through the highs and lows, that night will be in the back of my mind forever.
I later learned that a certain David Platt and Geoff Thomas lined up for Crewe that night, who'd have thought that they'd have gone onto win England caps years after they witnessed Northampton Town win the Fourth Division title? I am also pleased after all these years to still see my good friend Lee Wade at Sixfields, still a loyal Cobbler like myself. I'm sure Richard Hill's goal was acted out over and over again in the school yard that term. Finally, I was a fully-fledged Cobbler!

**I had cracked it now**

The summer holidays of 1987 flew by as I knew I had cracked it now. There was no trouble, I didn't get beaten up and finally going to the County Ground would be on my weekly agenda. I could make that short trip along Collingwood Road or Oakwood Road, cross over Abington Avenue, buying a programme from the lad on the corner and wander through the gates into the ground.

The following season in Division Three started with a flyer as Chester City were crushed 5-0 at Sealand Road before a huge crowd turned out to watch a 1-1 draw in the first home game of the season. Trevor Morley scored with a diving header in the 88th minute, but a deserved win was snatched away when veteran Gerry Armstrong equalised five minutes into injury time. I was there this time; it was my second game. A school mate left with five minutes to go and thought the game ended 0-0 until he heard the score the following day.

The momentum carried on that season as the goals continued, although not quite as freely as the previous season but we had some crazy games. Hallowe'en at Aldershot, Cobblers led 2-0, 3-1 and 4-2 but it ended 4-4.

The funniest chant of this season was in the home v Fulham. Town lead 3-1 thanks to an opener from Tony Adcock. Dave Gilbert got the second with a stunning cross/volley from the touch line which keeper Jim Stannard somehow dropped over the line. Paul Culpin scored a cracking volley for the third. At this point the Hotel End started chanting "You should've gone to the boat race" to the Fulham fans. It was funny at the time.

As the season drew on, we did get a little excited about reaching the play offs and I remember we needed to win our final two games to make sure. The last home game was against Blackpool and it was a topsy turvy affair. After a goal less first half, the visitors scored first before both sides swapping leads and Tony Adcock equalised for 3-3 in the last minute. We needed to beat Sunderland at Roker Park to have any further hope, but we lost 3-1 to the Champions and were pipped by Bristol City.

**My first season ticket**

My first season ticket was proudly in my hand as I wandered through the gate of the Family Enclosure for the start of the 1988/89 season. Mum treated me to it for my birthday but what I didn't realise was that it didn't cover cup games. After the 1-0 opening win over Brentford, I walked up to the turnstile three days later to watch the Littlewoods Cup game against Colchester, only to be turned away. Luckily, living so close to the ground I was able to run home and smash open my piggy bank and run back to the ground only to hear a massive cheer and realised I had missed the first goal. Four more followed though as Town won 5-0.

Things started to look rosy that season, on the first of October we beat Aldershot 6-0, with five of the goals coming in the last 25 minutes. We looked like world beaters but nine defeats from the next ten games followed and we plummeted towards the danger zone.

The eleventh game in the sequence was against Wolves at home, the league leaguers looked to be showing no remorse against any opposition and a large crowd turned out for the Sunday showdown. It was a cracker as Wayne Williams curled in a thirty yarder for the opener, Dean Thomas lashed home a pile driver from twenty yards to make it 2-1 and Tony Adcock put the icing on the cake to secure a 3-1 win. That was it for highlights that season. Aside from another six-goal thriller with Blackpool, a 4-2 win this time, we signed off the season with a 2-3 home defeat to Bolton and finished one place above relegation.

**End of an era**

For some reason we never really recovered and the following season the bubble finally burst. We were relegated and Graham Carr quit as manager. It was a shame as the first half of the season was a non-entity and we sort of plodded along in mid-table. We had high hopes in the new year though as a FA Cup run suddenly woke us all up.

The first round draw paired us with Kettering Town. Talk about a local derby or what? This was to be my first away game and boy was I excited? The home side gave us a few early scares but in the end Dean Thomas's long-range effort was enough to see us through. It could have been more if it hadn't been for some wasteful finishing. It was still great watching the highlights on Match of the Day though.

The second round brought non-league Aylesbury to the County Ground, but we needed a replay and extra time before a Bobby Barnes goal saw us through. Next up was Coventry City, the 1987 FA Cup winners! The Sky Blues had been embarrassed by Sutton United the season after they won it and now it was our turn to dish out the giant-killing.

**A real buzz**

There was a real buzz around as we arrived at the ground at one o clock, an hour and a half earlier than normal. I can't remember why we got there so early, but there were already more people in the ground then than there was for a league game. A load of us perched ourselves in our now regular spot in the middle of the Hotel End, just in front of the singers. By kick off, you couldn't move! It was throwing it down with rain and the visitors looked less than impressed with the state of the pitch as they ran out. Early in the game the Hotel End was cheering as Bobby Barnes's shot beat keeper Steve Ogrizavic, but the ball hit the post and came back out. It took a few minutes for word to go around that we hadn't actually scored. A couple of minutes before half time though, Steve Berry turned home Bobby Barnes cross and the mother of all goal celebrations happened. It didn't stop until well after half time.

Coventry were shell shocked, they looked so uncomfortable on the muddy pitch as their danger men Cyrille Regis and Dave Bennett struggled to get the ball under control. In the final minutes, it was hard to tell which colour shirt was which as the players were so caked in mud. The final whistle celebrations were wild, but police and stewards prevented us from running onto the pitch, so we had the stay in the Hotel End. Probably just as well, because the pitch resembled something like a recent Glastonbury Festival at that point. Somebody actually stole the kit after the game, but after an appeal in the Chronicle & Echo it turned up. I think a dog called *'Pickles'* found it. Either that, of it turned up in a hedge.

**That was that**

The giant killing of Coventry was to be our season as poor weather put pay any momentum, in fact we played something like two games in seven weeks and one of those was a disappointing fourth round exit at Rochdale. Around 3,500 Cobblers made the trip to Spotland and the home side had a day to remember. I have written for the Rochdale programme a couple of times and the guy I know there, Mark, always reminds me of that January day. Thanks for that!

We were finally relegated at Tranmere on the last but one game of the season. All my school mates had now returned to wearing their Liverpool scarves and the Mickey taking began.

Well there's a few of my early Cobblers memories, it's time to hand you over to some fellow Cobblers. Here are some great memories of the County Ground days and why these people became Cobblers fans.

*The players celebrate the win over Coventry with some bubbly. They couldn't afford champagne, so they had to make do with cans of Carlsberg lager. (Pete Norton)*

# Lost Shoes and Ripped Trousers

I guess I had an early feel for football as my dad never missed a chance to watch it when it was on television. My first memory of watching a football match was the 1978 FA Cup Final between Ipswich Town and Arsenal. Mum was sent out shopping and was told not to return before 5pm!

**He hated Paul Mariner**

When England matches were on television, my brother and I were allowed to watch providing we were silent. For some unknown reason to myself, my dad had this hatred for Ipswich Town striker Paul Mariner, and before a World Cup Qualifier he had threatened to urinate over the television should he score. Yep, you guessed it, Mariner scored against Hungry to put us into the World Cup Finals, so come the final whistle the deed was done, as the television went bang my mum dived for cover somewhat outraged.

Another time Ray Kennedy fell over and gave away a goal against Italy. At the top of his voice Dad yelled, "Get up Kennedy you big useless turd!" My brother and I burst into fits of laughter and were soon sent to bed.

On another occasion, when the Home Internationals were played, Dad feigned illness so we could return from holiday early, and he could watch England beat Scotland 3-1. Not satisfied with just the win, he took my brother and I to the bridge across the Motorway, at the Newport Pagnell Service area, to give the returning Scottish fans in their buses the v-sign as they headed back up North.

**Penalty save in front of the Hotel End**

As a yearly birthday present my Uncle Roger took me to a Cobblers match, gratefully, my birthday fell on FA Cup first round day. I first ventured through the County Ground turnstiles in 1982 and witnessed a 0-0 draw against Peterborough United, with goalkeeper Neil Freeman saving a penalty in front of The Hotel End.

My first real memory of the ramshackle old County Ground, was the smell of Ralgex drifting out from the changing rooms. Another year, I saw us beat Wimbledon 3-2, and remember a supporter being thrown into the back of the net in a mad celebration.

As I went through my teens, I travelled from Wolverton to Northampton by train. I was there that evening we won the old Fourth Division Title beating Crewe Alexandra 2-1, where believe it or not, little did we know that one of the mascots who led out the team that night, was to be camp comic Alan Carr. Once the final whistle had blown the annual invasion onto the pitch time came, so in my haste I scaled the fence and managed to shred my trousers in the process. Travelling back home minus my trousers got me some odd looks I can tell you, as I walked back to the train station. And having to explain how I'd managed it to a somewhat bemused Dad was even worse. Another time, being a supporter of superstition, I would take my usual spot on the Hotel End with a cup of Bovril and hot dog in hand, when a pre match shot by Phil Chard missed the goal, and smashed into me, thus spilling my Bovril and hot dog all over me. Phil gave me an apologetic wave as all around me laughed.

Being the eldest brother of three, I took my younger brother and teach him the joys of supporting The Cobblers. For a while if he could fit under the turnstiles and was allowed free admission. Throughout time each and everyone one of us has a story they would rather forget, but others won't let you and bring it up every time there's a family get together.

Early one January we played Barnet and drew 1-1. In my excitement being in a crowd surge, I somehow lost one of my shoes. Once the celebrations had died down, I yelled out loudly if anyone had seen my shoe? A voice from the back of the Hotel End yelled back "Here it is." To this day I am still confused as to how my shoe had managed to travel backwards and upwards? My shoe went up in the air and I've never seen it again. If you happen to have acquired a light brown Hush Puppy size 9, please can I have it back? Again, a somewhat cumbersome walk back to the train station and again a bemused dad had to be told of how I'd lost another item of clothing, while supporting my beloved Cobblers.

**Supermac bought me a pint**

The big day came when I passed my driving test, and there was no stopping me, as I would follow my beloved Cobblers over land, sea and Barnet. I went to Crewe one Tuesday Night and saw our then saviour, Michael McRitchie, and yelled out, "Supermac" who proceeded to buy me and a few others a drink or three.

The wettest I have ever been, had to be one Saturday when we played away at Chesterfield. We won 2-1 thanks to a late goal by Steve Terry, and despite the rain we all went delirious, as we had been on a bad run on and off the field. My abiding memory of the day, was watching then fanzine editor Rob Marshall run down the almost empty terrace with his sheepskin coat and perm going as fast as his feet could take him.

One Friday lunchtime whilst driving home for lunch, it was announced on the radio that we had sacked Theo Foley and twelve other players, which almost had me driving through the front of Newport Pagnell Fire Station! The next day, we were scheduled to play Barnet away, and I wanted to be there to support whatever team we could put out that day. The only problem was that I didn't finish work until 2pm, but incredibly my unreliable Mini Metro didn't let me down and I was there applauding the lads on with a few minutes to spare before kick off.

As the County Ground's floodlights went out for the very last time ever, I thought to myself, what was the one abiding memory I would take with me. It has to be of a fellow supporter who stood close to me called Bill. A Scotsman with a beard who always had me in fits of laughter, when he often yelled out, "Thank goodness I'm wearing my brown trousers."

Early one season we played Leyton Orient in the League Cup away, and after leaving Euston Station I came across a tramp who hassled me for change, but I chose to ignore. Spotting my team shirt, scarf and hat, he wished us bad luck. We lost 5-0. On the way home I decided to try and find the said tramp and unforgivably I gave him a bloody good hiding, sorry Mr Tramp!

One Friday night we played York City away, and somehow our driver managed to lose his way. We flagged down a York City supporter who was happy to give us directions, that was until he released, (much to his horror once on our bus) we were Cobblers Supporters!

I always said as a kiddie, I would buy a house overlooking the County Ground, so I could watch my beloved Cobblers for free, but then we moved to Sixfields. As much as I love Sixfields, I guess it's just not the same as the County Ground Days. I do miss my pre match pee in Abington Park!

One Saturday we played Bournemouth, and a certain Jermaine Defoe scored a hat trick against us. As I was leaving the stands, I bumped into

Mel Machin, who was at the time Director of Football at Bournemouth, and said to him, how well I thought Defoe ripped us apart. He replied, "Mark my words he will be a very big player in the future."

I saw the happiness and sadness of how Wembley can be, from the euphoria of a win to the abject misery of a very quiet train ride back home, the latter of which I don't want to ever feel again, ever.

As a Cobblers Supporter I grew up expecting us to lose week in week out, but now at Sixfields we win more than we lose these days. Admittedly as I've aged, the price of football has gone up, and I've got responsibilities so I can't go week in, week out. But because of that, when I can get along to matches it makes it all that much more special. Especially as my beloved Cheryl (the current Mrs Tyro, god I hope she's the last, I'm getting exhausted!) who is a closet Tottenham Hotspur fan, likes to sit beside me but only to my right hand side as it's become a superstitious ritual...it also saves kissing her goodbye when she tags along!

**I gained a rogue of a reputation**

With the invention of the internet, getting to know supporters was interesting to say the least, and I gained and still do, a somewhat rogue of a reputation online. One day it was suggested we organise a bus, so we could all get together. The Big Day Out arrived and we set off for Yeovil. At the time I was married, and the wife hated football with a passion. Occasionally though she would ask to accompany me to matches. Her first match was against Millwall which she managed to fall asleep through! For weeks she had moaned at me for wanting to go on a bus trip for an away game and the night before she decided she would like to go. After begging the trip organiser for a spare seat, we managed to squeeze her in (a big challenge if you had even seen her a*** I tell you!) she was coming along.

**Headache**

Close to Yeovil we had the pre match pint at a very nice pub with food laid on, but she had decided to go around a local charity shop and generally not join in with the pre match banter. Even worse, once at the ground she informed me that she had a headache, and didn't want to watch the game, so I had to bribe the bus driver to let her stay on the bus while the match was being played. I don't like to admit it but that day I realised, sadly my marriage was coming to an end. Various photographs of the day were put up on the Hotel End website and one showing me and the wife talking while sitting on a wall, (I say talking, it was actually an argument) this showed my marriage going south.

**A 1-1 draw took second place that day**

Even though we had got a credible 1-1 draw that day, football took a second place as I searched my heart for answers. Thankfully the day ended upbeat as not once, twice, but three times on the trot, I won various stuffed toys in a grab machine, at the stop at the service station on the way back home. With a crowd around me, the cheers got louder and louder as my good luck continued, that was until we were ushered away by security, and told to keep the noise down to a dull roar. Being the big-hearted fella I am, I gave the toys I had won to Marvo and Linda, who had organised the bus trip that day, (much to the disgust of my wife).

As time has gone on, I've always given Linda Smith donations to various raffles and prize draws that she has organised on behalf of many Cobblers fans organisations and she has become a good friend.

I finally got lucky and won the opportunity to present Mark Bunn with the Hotel End Message Board Player of The Season Trophy in 2006/07. It was very interesting to see how the players train.

Well that's some of my memories of supporting Northampton Town. There are many, many more, yet not enough energy to write them all down, maybe one day when I write the complete Tyro Autobiography!

**Stewart Bailey (a.k.a.Tyringham1)**

*(Pete Norton)*

# Hooked by the Hotel End (The Lost Shoe Again)

My first memory of following the Cobblers would have to be a home game with Barnet in 1991, it was an FA Cup Second Round Replay at the County Ground, the first game ended 0-0 at Underhill. Unfortunately, the Cobblers were robbed in the replay with Barnet somehow running out 1-0 winners with the crappiest of goals being scored in front of the Hotel End, how the ball somehow found its way into the net I will never know! Barnet were even reduced to 10 men during the game but the Cobblers just could not make the advantage pay and missing chance after chance. Don't get me wrong I can remember Barnet, who were then still a Conference side, defending resolutely throughout, it didn't matter what the Cobblers did, but it just wouldn't go in. Barnet always seemed to have someone on the line to prevent a Cobblers goal. This was the game when Cobblers fans first found their love affair of Barry Fry!

**Stuck in the mud**

The main and best thing about this game however did not come in the way of what was happening on the pitch, but on the famous Hotel End, as in one of many Cobblers attacks, the ball seemed to slowly role across the goal line and get stuck in the clogged up mud in the goalmouth, destined to go in we all thought as a mass surge seemed to come down from the back of the Hotel End with all ready to celebrate, unfortunately a Barnet defender managed to clear the ball yet again, but in the melee my older brothers shoe managed to come off his foot. Now imagine the moment, there you are standing on a packed Hotel End when someone lets out this "Where's My Shoe" at the top of his voice, it was almost as though everyone heard his cry and stopped to create space to search for this shoe. So forget the game for five minutes, a certain patch of the Hotel End was staring down towards the ground to look for this shoe, brilliant! Somehow though the shoe was discovered by a fellow supporter some way back from where we were standing that night. How this shoe had managed to travel back up the Hotel End remains a mystery, but it was a classic, hilarious moment and something which just won't be forgotten, and still has me in barrels of laughter to this day much to my brother's frustration.

I can clearly remember the build up to this game, arriving around the streets of Abington to park the car, looking up to see the light from the County Grounds floodlights illuminating the night sky, making the short walk up to the ground, I can remember there was definitely something in the air that night, with it being a night game and an FA Cup Second Round Replay, the atmosphere seemed great!

**The deafening chant**

Entering through the Hotel End turnstiles that night for a mere £3.00, I walked through the terrace with older members of my family around me, and this is the thing that has stuck with me ever since that night and is why I became hooked on Northampton Town Football Club from that moment onwards and why I still am now, as a very young and tiny ten year old attending his first ever football match, I was deafened by the chant which came down from the Hotel End. Everyone seemed to sing as I walked through them "NORTH...AMP...TONNNNNN, NORTHAMPTON, NORTHAMPTON...", you know the rest. Despite the result that night, I loved the experience of my first ever football match, I loved standing on that Hotel End as the years went by, even sitting right at the front for the first few seasons until I grew a little, the songs/chants that have remained with me ever since I loved, and like I say, I was hooked, maybe a name contender for the book Mark hey, "Hooked By The Hotel End!"

I can remember attending a few other matches that season, the Cobblers eventually ended 10th in the old Division Three with a poor run in, in which was a season that promised a lot to start off with, but off the field events with the club being put up for sale by Dick Underwood.

The following season, 1991/92 really got going for me, I would attend a lot of matches home and away with family and friends, some that spring to mind were another early season home game with a now league side in Barnet which ended 1-1, Bobby Barnes put the Cobblers in front, and once again despite looking comfortable Barnet levelled things up with virtually the last kick of the game, Gary Bull, brother of Steve with the goal. How they were becoming a bogey side for the Cobblers.

Burnley visited the County Ground in the November, Burnley actually p*ssed Division Three this season and run out 2-1 winners, their winner coming very late on to the delight of their large following that day. What sadly sticks in the mind from that day though was the match programme which was unfortunately nothing more than an A4 piece of paper which had been folded in half due to the ever-worsening financial situation at the County Ground.

**Give em the bird**

My very first away game arrived around this time also, a friend of the family took me on the coach to Rotherham to witness a 0-1 defeat, Steve Terry looping the ball into his own net to give Rotherham the points. I can remember as the coach arrived in Rotherham watching their fans make their way to the ground and asking those around me what I should do, to which I was given a response of give them the V sign with your two fingers. So there I was all of ten years old sticking my two fingers up through a coach window at Rotherham supporters, from their point of view it must have looked hilarious.

**Appeared in a book before**

One home game against Hereford proved to be quite pinnacle for myself actually that particular season, the game itself was dire and ended 1-1 but is was when supporters were stepping up efforts to oust the chairman from the club and were handing out red leaflets stating McRitchie Out which were to be held high as and when the Cobblers got a corner kick at the Hotel End, I seem to recall only one corner kick taken at that end of the ground that afternoon which seemed pretty typical of events at the time. Years later I was to find myself in one or two books about the club holding up one of these leaflets for the camera as I stand there. The books I have found myself in so far would be "It's All Cobblers To Me" and "Thanks For The Wembley's."

I can remember going to watch the Cobblers at several other places during this particular season, my family were pulling me out of school for the afternoon, mainly on a Tuesday just so that I could join them in going at away games. I loved this of course though. I remember travelling up to Scunthorpe where the Cobblers were easily beaten 0-3, there must have been 100 or so Cobblers fans there that night who just didn't stop singing. Is it me though or do the Cobblers just have an absolute dire record at Glanford Park?

I can remember making what seemed to be the longest of trips up to Burnley on a freezing cold evening in February or something to see Burnley demolish the Cobblers 5-0, Christian McLean was also sent off in this game. Burnley were flying high this season and the crowd was around 8,000, the Cobblers couldn't have had any more than a hardcore of around 50 fans stood on a massive open terrace that night. It was around 3.30am in the morning by the time my head hit the pillow, and with school the following morning! I wouldn't have changed it for the world though!

As the season wore on goals were proving hard to come by for the Cobblers with most of the squad now departed, it had been a good few games since the Cobblers had even scored, yet recorded a victory, so as luck would have it the next away game just had to be Carlisle away , another defeat by the score of 1-2 but the first goal had been scored under the Phil Chard era by a young Jimmy Benton.

Away at Barnet was a game that season which was memorable, on the Friday previous the Cobblers had announced that their entire first team had been either sacked or put up for sale, and that the team for Barnet on the Saturday would be mainly made up of youth team players, as we made our way down the M1/M25 that day there seemed to be Cobblers fans in car after car and coach after coach descending on Barnet. It is amazing that when your team has some bad news, and their backs are against the wall that the fans come out in support, the Cobblers must have had a good thousand or so packed into that side terrace at Underhill that afternoon, the team went down 0-3, to be honest it was an easy win for Barnet, the team battled hard but created very little. The players at the end came over and thanked the support they were given that afternoon. Things boiled over a little upon leaving the ground that day with a few Cobblers and the police, emotions were running high for your most hardened Cobblers fans that day it seemed.

As the seasons went on, I would attend on a regular basis with my older brother and other family members home and away to watch the Cobblers. I attended the very last game at the County Ground against Mansfield Town, which to be honest wasn't quite the same as the previous final home game against Chester City it has to be said, but at least I can say I was there, a sad evening in many ways but the start of a new chapter for the club. I miss the Hotel End, but I like Sixfields, it has potential and the sooner it is re-developed the better, for the sake of the club, although atmosphere wise there is absolutely no comparison between the Hotel End and the West Stand, I think you will agree.

**Agony and ecstasy**

I have travelled far and wide to watch the Cobblers and have notched up a fair few grounds in my time. I have experienced pretty much every emotion that comes with being a football supporter I guess, from the ecstasy of Swansea to the devastation of Grimsby both at Wembley.

To sum things up then, I did not choose to support Northampton Town, I was born in Northampton so the Cobblers found me. I remain as loyal and as dedicated to the Cobblers as I have always been and always will be, as is my older brother and my children will be too. Only earlier this week were myself and my daughter in the club shop kitting her out for the new season. Supporting the Cobblers fills me with a sense of pride and passion, which if I am honest is more than what can be said about the few people I know who now, despite once claiming they were Cobblers fans now choose to follow a franchised club twenty minutes down the M1. It proves how fickle football supporters can be I guess, but surely when this team and it's pathetic excuse of supporters walk through the away turnstiles at Sixfields this coming season, they will all glance across and say to themselves that oh yeah, I once followed them and actually used to enter through that side of the ground! I know that Peterborough will always be far and away Northampton's main rivals, the Dons although they mightily annoy me, I cannot take seriously as a football club. Give me Northampton any day!

**Len Bailey**

# Corby, Saints or Cobblers

Hello to all you Cobblers fans, I can tell you a little tale regarding following my team, Bury, if you like.

It was a Tuesday night match towards the end of the season and it coincided with me being on a course from work for the week in Milton Keynes. I finished for the day at 5pm so had plenty of time to get to the match for a 7.30pm kick off.

The match was being played at the old cricket ground, but I thought I'll easily find it, floodlights and all that. Directions were never my strong point, as you will soon find out! I found myself on high ground overlooking Northampton and, in the distance, I could see floodlights, so I aimed for them. It was now 6.40pm giving me plenty of time to reach my destination. Unfortunately, when I got there the streets were very quiet and as I passed the ground it was obviously not the right one. There was an old bloke walking along and I asked him where I was. "Corby Town" he answered and then gave me directions to get to Northampton, although a combination of them not being very good and my directional sense would add to the drama of finding my destination.

It was now 6.50pm and the daylight was fading fast, but in the distance I could see floodlights, so again I aimed for them. People were milling about and so I parked up and walked in the direction of the ground. One thing I noticed was the lack of fans wearing colours, but I got into the queue only to look over the gate and spot... rugby posts. I was at Northampton's rugby ground. Oh no! So I walked up to the commissionaire and told him my predicament. He found it very funny and decided to bellow out at the top of his voice, "Hey lads there's a guy here from Bury who's come to the wrong ground." He couldn't stop laughing but I wasn't too amused, especially as his onward directions were bobbins too.

**Almost there**

7.10pm and I went back to the car and went in the general direction he had given me. I got on a road out of town, but there was not a soul about. Then I spied someone in their garden, stopped and ran back. He pointed me onward and finally I was heading towards the County Ground. At 7.45pm I finally arrived and passed all the parked cars only to find there was no space near the ground, so I had to turn around and drive about half a mile away again. It was then kick off time and I set off running back to the ground and got there just after kick off. I asked a policeman where the away supporters' entrance was and he replied "Right on the opposite side of the ground and it's a cricket ground, so a hell of a long way mate." He must have felt so sorry for me that he told me to go in the closest turnstile and he would escort me round inside the ground. The kiosk guy told him he couldn't let me in as the prices were different for away supporters and he had cashed up anyway, so the cop told me to climb over the turnstile and pay £5, which I did.

If I thought that my night couldn't get much worse, just as I was climbing over there was a big cheer. Northampton had scored. I walked round to the back of the goal with the other Bury supporters to watch the remainder of the game, that ended up 1-0 to the Cobblers. To say my first experience of Northampton wasn't my best one, but it has made quite a few people laugh. Good luck to the Cobblers.

**Jack Berry - Bury Fan**

*The real County Ground (Bobby the Cobbler)*

# My Dad's Influence

Ron Page (1923-2005) and Jeff Hardman in terms of football at the very least, were and are my biggest influences. Lifelong 'Gooners' and 'Trotters' fans respectively, both were responsible for my unconditional love of Northampton Town FC. I was born in Northampton in 1968 but my dad's wanderlust took us as a family to all corners of our disaffected homeland never returning to live in a house with an NN postcode.

**Unfortunately for him, my brother Jase was born in Swindon**

I was hooked on football from an early age. My dad took me to trials and coaching schools and I would play with mates until it was so dark you couldn't see the ball. I was also particularly fascinated by the Classified Check. Around the 1975/76 season I heard my gramp shout out with delight when his beloved Arsenal had beaten North London rivals Spurs, the intensity of his delight fuelled by the fact that my nan was a big Spurs fan. This prompted me to ask him why he supported the Arsenal and his answer changed my life. "You support the team from where you were born." From that moment I was a Cobbler. Unfortunately for him, my brother Jase was born in Swindon.

Of course, the other rule is that you support your dad's team but my dad made a fatal schoolboy error. He took me to see the Cobblers first in 1977 away to Southport before trying to tempt me with Second Division football at Burnden Park when the likes of Frankie Worthington, Willie Morgan and Peter Dunne were playing. Fair play, it was quality football at the time but all I could think about was George Reilly missing a sitter against Southport in that 3-1 defeat. Consequently, pocket money was converted into postal orders and sent to the Club Shop in exchange for programmes, key rings, badges, rosettes and Bob Thomas player pics.

**We lost 6-0**

A move to the Medway Towns followed where I spent most of my school years. This was a surprisingly productive time for me as a Cobblers supporter, games against Gillingham were a regular occurrence and two of my favourite memories relate to this era. In retrospect, my dad must have been really conscious of my Cobblers obsession. I'm not so sure, having broken the main rule of who you should support with my own children (all Boltonians), if I could be as supportive as my dad was of me. He constantly pulled out the stops for me. In around 1980 he arranged it for me to be a ball boy at a Cobblers reserve game at Gillingham's Garrison Ground. He had done this through the Gillingham and Republic of Ireland player Damian Richardson. We lost 6-0 but to have a team photo with the likes of Maurice Muir and Adam Sandy either side of me kept me awake for days! I also remember Dennis Byatt and Clive Walker being particularly kind to me that day if not a little bemused by their superstar status.

**A starkers Ian Benjamin held his hand out**
Over the years I got to see the first team many times at the Priestfield Stadium. Following some cheeky correspondence to the Club they invited me into the dressing room following the first leg of a League Cup game in the 1986/87 season. Graham Carr was a true gentleman and introduced me to the players. A starkers Ian Benjamin got out of the bath and held out his hand. I still occasionally wake up in a cold sweat imagining how that could have gone so wrong. For the return leg at the County Ground I blagged a seat on a Gillingham Supporters coach wearing my colours. As luck would have it the coach was full of middle-aged women (and men) with bad perms. I returned home with a straight nose and ribs intact. Tony Cascarino was probably the difference between the two sides that night. As time went on, I occasionally took the train from Chatham to Victoria, hopped across the Underground to Euston and journeyed to Northampton before the long walk up to the Hotel End.

I moved to Canterbury after that and met the missus Keren. Post student poverty took me back almost full-circle to Bolton in 1995 where a house could be purchased for half a shandy and a bag of pork scratchings. Through the Cobblers Fanzine What a Load of Cobblers I met up with a vicar called Peter (featured in 4-4-2 once) who lived in Bury. We attended a few games together including that glorious victory over Swansea at Wembley. The Cobblers at Wembley! Even Pete Norton can't believe we played at Wembley. "One Pete Norton, there's only one Pete Norton..."

Our eldest son Christian was born in 1998 and began going to games while still in nappies. Travelling to one particular game upped the ante considerably. It was the last game of the season in 2002/03 away at Mansfield. Already relegated we were playing to avoid bottom place. As we drove along the M61, the passengers in both cars did a double take as we each clocked Northampton Town scarves in the back window. We took turns in overtaking, checking each other out before coming off at a service station. Casual as you like we swapped phone numbers and continued on down to Mansfield together. Turns out Michael Sullivan and family live six miles away and we've been travelling to matches together ever since averaging around 35/40 games a season. For me that's a dream come true and I owe Michael a lot. It also needs mentioning that his mum Anne is the Queen of Kingsthorpe and purveyor of quality pre-match fry-ups.

**Foolishly Keren thought Saturdays would be chick flicks and chocolate**

Our youngest son Daniel joined the gang and foolishly Keren thought her Saturdays would be chick flicks and chocolate. Instead she's glued to Sky Sports checking out what mood we're gonna be in when we get home.

As I said, I broke my Gramp's rule when it came to my own son's and now daughter Janie. By rights they should be Bolton fans but I got in early learning from my Dad's mistake. I watch them at football training at Fred Longworth School in Tyldesley (Ashley Westwood's old school). Every kid is wearing a Manchester United or Bolton kit and there's Christian and Dan in the Claret and White...not being Campo or Ronaldo. Nah! They're 'Titch' or 'Cokey' and proud of it. The Cobblers are everything.

**Paul Hardman aka auntie**

*Paul's scrapbook from 1980-81 season (we all had one)*

# Picking My Nose

I have very fond memories of Northampton Town FC. My first memories were as a ball boy at the old County Ground in 1982 when I used to get paid the princely sum of 50p a game and was forced to wear a shiny, bright, purple tracksuit. Many a time I would get a cheer as a ball was thumped out across the cricket pitch and I would slip on my backside trying to retrieve it. It seemed as though in them days the club could only afford one match ball and unless it went into the bowling club, I had to get up, compose myself, unable to bury my face and do a 100 metre sprint to retrieve it.

I also recall when me and my old mate Lee Arnold bunked off school to 'ball boy' a reserve match. We told our parents we had been given permission by the school, only to hear "Oi, what are you two doing here" from Lee's dad in the stand. Taken by the ears, we were driven back to school and frog marched into the Headmaster's office to explain ourselves. I still see Lee's dad at Sixfields now and he still gives me a wry smile. Another game that sticks in my mind was being ball boy for the home FA Cup tie against Aston Villa when Mark Walters scored the best goal I remember at The County Ground. I was so excited knowing that the highlights were on Match of the Day that night, telling all my mates at school to watch it. Waiting with baited breath, the team names came on the screen and there I was on camera, PICKING MY NOSE!

**The glitz and glamour of football**

I always wanted some kind of connection with the club, playing for the Town Boys and hoping to emulate my heroes of the day, John Buchannen and Steve Phillips. The closest I got next was working for Tony Ansell in his burger bar behind the Hotel End. It was a strange smell and I can still recall it today. The smell of burning onions, blended with the stench of urine from the 30-foot hole in the ground covered by a wall, known as the men's toilet, oh what happy memories. Tony's pay was not that good (he had to make his fortune somehow), and I remember trudging tins of burgers and sausages to his café on Abington Park, hiding them in a bush and scoffing them till I threw up on the way home. Perks of the job I suppose!

My career as a footballer never paid off so it was then onto supporting the lads from the terraces in the eighties and nineties. My favourite players of those times were Trevor Morley, Eddie McGoldrick, Dean Thomas, Phil Chard, Martin Aldridge, Ian Sampson and Ray Warburton and the best manager by far was Graham Carr. I travelled up and down the country and win, lose or draw, we would be there next game. The saddest time was going into receivership, but still recall our next game, the trip to Barnet. The best away game for vocal support I remember my throat still suffers to this day.

**A brand new start**

Having spent so long watching the Cobblers at the ramshackle County Ground I was in awe watching Sixfields being built and would photograph it through the different building stages. Finally, when the stage was set goose pimples formed when we kicked off. My best memory at Sixfields was when Martin Aldridge volleyed the ball into the North Stand net and did his backward summersault. I had a feeling it would be the start of good things to come. They did and the Wembley memories I will treasure forever and with the club on a better financial footing the only way is up. But I will always look back at my time at the County Ground and realise how lucky we are now. But what good fun it was then.

Martin Wade

*Martin celebrates promotion in 2004 (Pete Norton)*

## The Love Affair Begins

Born in 1974 and brought up in Northampton, living for most of my childhood in Park Avenue North, it was only a matter of time before my football mad dad, took me down the road to Abington Avenue and introduced me to the wonderful world of Northampton Town - The Cobblers. My dad was fortunate enough to be in his youth during the swinging sixties to witness and fully appreciate the Cobblers dramatic rise and subsequent fall through the four divisions. It is some feat to go from Division Four to Division One and back again in the same decade, but that was exactly what happened of course. It is difficult to imagine what it would have been like seeing the Cobblers reaching the top-flight of English football. Despite having some newspaper clippings of this period and reading the book all about it, it still doesn't seem real. But it did happen, I was just eight years too late!

Unfortunately, during my lifetime, I haven't seen the club play at a level any higher than the third tier, which is where we are currently holding our own. I feel we are at the crossroads again in our history. Stadium re-development is key to our future I'm afraid. Get it and we can really push on and make a serious attempt to gain Championship status, fail to get it and the likelihood is we will continue to flirt between Leagues One and Two. That is for the future, but I want to look back on my twenty plus years as a Cobbler and how proud I am to be one.

It all started in the early eighties for me. I have very hazy recollections of my dad taking my brothers and me to a few games at the old County Ground to watch pretty poor Fourth Division football. I'm sure we were sometimes lifted over the turnstile after slipping the gateman a nice silver coin. Perhaps that's why the attendances were so small? We used to stand on the Spion Kop with what seemed about only twenty others, sometimes watching the action, sometimes playing our own game of football. To be honest, I wasn't really that interested in football at that age, but it got us out of the house and gave my mum a couple of hours peace on a Saturday afternoon. My dad wasn't as keen on it as he used to be either, perhaps understandable after the whirlwind of the sixties. The seventies and early eighties were fairly barren times. All that changed though for us in 1986. I was twelve years old and good friends with a certain Mark Kennedy.

In September of that year we returned back to Cherry Orchard Middle School and all of a sudden there was a lot of talk about how well the Cobblers were doing. Graham Carr was manager, exciting players had been recruited and there was optimism for the first time in ages. The first game I saw that season was on Tuesday October 22nd against Burnley. That was our sixth home win of the season and we had won the previous five. I remember walking the short distance to the ground with my dad and Jack, an old chap who lived up the road from us. There were plenty of likewise people and the talk was of how well we were doing and whether we could keep it going. We won this game 4-2 with two goals from Trevor Morley and one apiece from Ian Benjamin and Richard Hill in front of nearly 6,000 fans. We stood on the terrace next to the *'Meccano stand.'*

I talked my dad into taking us to the next game and that was four days later at home to Hereford. That was when I made my first appearance in the Hotel End, a big covered terrace that used to generate plenty of atmosphere. That was the place to be. We won this game 3-2 to make it seven home wins on the spin and 31 points out of a possible 36. And so it continued. The Cobblers continued to steamroller the opposition including scoring five against Rochdale, five at Crewe, six at Halifax, four against Exeter, Southend, Cardiff. It was a magical season. Crowds flocked to the County Ground. The clash against Cardiff City on December 28th attracted 11,138. The previous season the average was nearer the 2,000 mark. I remember treating myself to a seat in the temporary stand next to the Spion Kop for this game. I went with my dad as usual but bizarrely sat next to a Cardiff fan. An old boy who couldn't believe how good the Cobblers were and who was also dismayed at the Cardiff keeper being sent off. We won 4-1 and as ever were rampant.

The first game I went to without my dad was the final home game of the season against Crewe. A win would seal the Fourth Division title. I went with Mark Kennedy. He has already told this story elsewhere in this book so all I'll say is we won 2-1, Richard Hill scored the winner, which was his last ever goal for us in his last ever home game and we invaded the pitch to celebrate. A great night, one I will never forget. Seasons like that don't come around too often and I was glad to be a part of it, if a little young and naïve to perhaps fully appreciate it, but my love affair with the Cobblers was well and truly on.

**Lee Wade**

*Crowds flock back to the County Ground (Pete Norton)*

---

# What the Hell Am I Doing Here?

I this is a perfect question to fit the feeling you get on match day as a long-term Northampton Town fan. In a way, I think all Cobblers fans are a bit weird. Smack bang on a train line to London with likes of Chelsea, Tottenham and Arsenal on offer and they choose to follow a team which has been mediocre (and I'm being generous there) for the majority of its existence. It doesn't say much when your club is most famous for George Best scoring six past you and having a three-sided ground, with your pitch used as a car park for the adjoining cricket club in the summer. In fact, you can sum up being a Northampton supporter by watching the Cobblers goalie just lying on the floor for one of Georgie's six and facing the inevitable.

**My father was less pleased with me following the Cobblers**

Saying that, I must be one of the biggest weirdos. Growing up supporting Spurs in the very late eighties (after the glory years of Hoddle and Waddle of course), I became hooked by the Cobblers (didn't know how painful it could be!) after a school visit where we ran out onto the pitch at half time and proceeded to dribble balls through cones (no scrimping on the entertainment at the County Ground). Being a keen footballer myself, I was thrilled by the immediacy of the 'action' on the pitch and the chanting of the diehards in the Hotel End. My father on the other hand was less pleased with me going regularly to the Cobblers. It wasn't that he disliked football or anything like that but more that he didn't want me following such a sh*t team. Looking back, he had a point.

The year was 1992 and things were bad on and off the pitch. Actually, they were terrible on and off the pitch. The club went into administration, sacking nine players and the management team, there were public meetings and fans baying for the blood of the despised chairman Michael McRitchie. On the pitch, a backs to the wall fight was on our hands in nearly every game, seven consecutive defeats, the threat of the Conference and possible oblivion hanging over us. And I couldn't get enough of it. Perhaps all this upheaval and grief was exciting to me as a young lad. Whilst there were loads of older Cobblers fans who were desperately worried about what was going to happen to their team, I was buzzing of the excitement of a relegation battle, watching mediocre players fighting tooth and nail to stay in the league and laughing at all these grim faced Northamptonians collecting pennies in buckets outside the County Tavern.

**He suddenly became more open to me attending matches**

Now that the Cobblers were fighting for survival, my father (being a leftie) suddenly became more open to me attending matches so that I could relay all the rumours that were flying around about the future of the club. He even found himself at the front of the famous Exeter Rooms meeting where he and his mates were pushing for the Council to construct an Italian style Stadio Communale for us to play in. That said, he would usually never come in to the ground, preferring to drop us off and have a pint in the Abington Park Hotel whilst the match went on. Afterwards, he would laugh like a drain about seeing the ball flying three hundred feet in the air every ten seconds and commenting that the local residents in Abington Avenue had to put special roof tiles on their houses to protect them from the football projectiles that the less than skillful Northampton defenders had launched into space.

**Playing for their careers**
Not that I cared that much. I had a sense of humour about it all. Yes, Northampton had loads of crap players. But they were crap players playing for their careers. There was a sense of desperate pride around the place that only those that were there at the time can put into words. Imagine being a punk in the days of the Pistols or the Clash and being told your music is crap. Yeah it might be crap but it's my music and it represents me. In the same way the Cobblers players represented us. A lot of the players were poor, past it or barely out of short trousers, but they were keeping afloat a fast sinking ship, often going without proper pay. I respected them for that. To be fair, there were a few half decent players in amongst the trash. Take for instance, Mickey Bell, a tricky winger who went on to have a good career, Steve Brown, a no-nonsense centre mid who became a bit of a cult figure at Wycombe and the late Martin Aldridge who gave us that little bit of hope with his forward runs. Forgive me if my memories of this time come across as disjointed, it is nearly twenty years ago now (scary) and my thoughts have become more dreamlike than my memories of Sixfields (which I can put in a rough timeline). I remember standing on the cricket side against Hereford (a team forever sponsored by Sun Valley and with loads of bald players). They had four players sent off but we could still only manage a draw. God knows what happened that game. It must have been like King Canute holding back the waves or perhaps (if my dad is to be believed) our players were more interested in seeing how high they could spoon the ball into the sky. "Fifty quid says I can hit the roof of number 56." An FA Cup game against non-league Bromsgrove, where me and my friend missed the bus and had to walk in the rain from Weston Favell Centre. Of course, we lost. There were good times too though. Take the game against Mansfield. Standing under the floodlight at the entrance to the Hotel End on a dark night and seeing us stuff the Notts team 5-1. It seemed like football

perfection and I swear that the man in the headband Steve Terry lobbed the goalie for one of the goals. We all thought that we would murder the league after that (did we f**k). Efon Elad our Cameroonian international (yeah right!) running like Forest Gump on speed but not knowing how to shoot. Kevin Wilkin's long-range goal in the last game (not) at the County Ground and towards the end Ray Warburton winning headers for fun.

In the end it was only right that we moved on. Our home was killing us. We couldn't go on being such a joke. When you mention the Cobblers and people laugh, it was those years around 1992 that did it. We were awful. But as a supporter, I believe you should take the rough with the smooth. Those bitter years at the County Ground made all the Wembley success that little bit sweeter. I can understand why grown men cried when John Frain curled in his free kick in the 93rd. We had moved on and we could never go back. It doesn't stop us missing it though!

**Tom Reed**

*Watching a match from the Spion Kop. (Tranmere on Tour)*

# Norm Enders Memories

As a regular at the County Ground in my school years, I have many fond memories of standing on the famous Hotel End, passing away many Saturdays and cold Tuesday evenings watching the Cobblers win, lose and draw. Having moved away from Northampton a few years ago and travelling around various places in this world, I have only loosely followed the Town's fortunes over the past few years, but the memories are still close to my heart. Here are a few to share with you from the late eighties.

**My most embarrassing personal Cobblers moment**

It was my first trip onto the Spion Kop. I don't know how I got on there as I wasn't a member of the Kop. As far as I remember I was, at the time, a family enclosure member (less atmosphere and life than the Kop, but more than the Cricket Side) but a regular on the Hotel End. It was the first game after Tony Adcock's departure and it was against Preston North End. Of course, the Kop was right next to *'The Cage'*, which housed the away fans and we had to endure the constant droning of the euro-pop like hit, "P-N-EEEEEEEEEEEEEEE, P-N-EEEEEEEEEEEEEEE..." We were also enduring a lacklustre performance from a side that was yet to be graced with Bobby Barnes. No striker, a poor game and a song only slightly better than S-Club 7. Not a good start.

The pivotal moment came when the Cobblers won a penalty in front of the Hotel End. Until his departure Tony had always slotted those home, but with him gone who would fill that exalted position? My heart leapt with joy as Dean Thomas, the great 'Deano', stepped up to the mark. That settled it! It was a cert! We had won the game, the league, the FA and World Cups! Heck, we had probably won the respect of Jimmy Hill... maybe not. Anyway, Deano was going to take a penalty. He was a master of the direct free kick. He had put in some great goals from well outside the penalty area that one from the spot... it was there! I was so delighted; I decided to share my joy with the now downtrodden and silent Preston Fans. I began jumping up and down, pointing at them and screaming, "That's you sorted, Deano's gonna get this, you've lost now" and so on. They seemed to take on board what I was saying, and I quite admired the way they took the news of their impending defeat.

Back to the action on the pitch, Deano placed the ball on the spot. He may as well just put it in the back of the net now, I was thinking, and backed up to face down the keeper. "Why doesn't he and the rest of his team just concede, why don't they go home and disband" and....

The following week's issue of What a Load of Cobblers fanzine (WALOC) asked this question: A Dean Thomas penalty is most likely to break:

a) The back of the net?
b) The spirit of every Cobblers fan?
c) The skull of some poor shopper in the market square?

A save? Acceptable! A miss? Heart breaking, but manageable! Clearing the crossbar? Gareth Southgate! But clearing the Hotel End barely even touching the roof? I can never go to Preston for the rest of my life, they have long memories.

**Someone else's most embarrassing moment**

Despite the above, I can take comfort from one thing, that I wasn't the person that I am about to mention. At least I can go to Coventry with some confidence. Why Coventry? Because this person's eternal shame came during the memorable FA Cup Third Round VICTORY against the then-top-flight Coventry City. It was a day of pride, except for one bloke.

The County Ground was packed. I don't know for sure, but I would imagine it had never been so full since the legendary visit of George Best. More importantly, the Hotel End was heaving and you'd have thought that it would have been a time for people to exercise their right to come up with a memorable and lasting put down of the opposition. It was the time to become a Hotel End legend. For one man the pressure was just too much. With Coventry shooting towards the Kop, we had Coventry's keeper, Steve Ogrizovic at our mercy. He should have left a broken man doubting his ability, his sexuality and his parentage. He left unaware of his true status in any of these areas. One middle-aged gentleman, a front-of-the-Hotel-End Ender, made his bid for glory, shouting time and time again, "Ogrizovic, you Tory!" It never caught on. Even in the modern game no keeper has had to suffer the broadcasting of their political preferences by opposition fans. I wonder why?

**Coach drivers**

Another FA Cup game, but this one marking my first trip away from home to Barnet. I travelled, along with Mark, on a Mounties coach (why was it called the Mounties, I don't know, some Canadian connection maybe?) This gave us the honour of being the youngest Mounties members by about 50 years. To cut a long story short, as we pulled into the approach road to the Barnet ground a car was trying to exit that same road. You really have to admire the skill of a professional coach driver. Not only did he hit the car, he also got it stuck under the left front wheel arch and pushed it about 10 metres back down the road. Its memories like this that make life worth living.

**That's what you call gratitude**

Something that never ceases to amaze me is the lack of gratitude that some players show to their former clubs. I mean, a player under performs, gets mercilessly sold to another club, that club plays the former club, and how does the returnee show his gratitude? By being on the winning side. Two cases stick in my memory as displays of total ingratitude.

I'll start with the game at which the memorable coach incident happened; Barnet. It was a FA Cup game that we should have won at the first attempt. I mean, they were part-timers, the "Back to work on Monday" crew. However, Cobblers were generous (there is no way that we played badly, does that ever happen?) and allowed Barnet to have an away-day at the County Ground to experience the better things in life... like playing on a cricket club car park. We couldn't fail in front of fortress Hotel End.

The returnee on this occasion was one Mickey Bodley. In the season that he came to the club he had been a delight to watch and seemed like he could be a Cobblers great. Unfortunately, he fell apart during the closed season due to the pressure of being in a low-division side. This led to another WALOC classic: "Would you buy a used football league career from Mickey Bodley?"

To take some of the pressure off the dear wee lad he was unloaded to the aforementioned part-timers. Of course, in his first game against his former club, there was some good-natured ribbing. I mean, the smile that must have come to him as he heard the fans that the previous season had sung his praises belt out the joyous refrain, "Cobblers reject." This smile melted into insignificance compared to the smile that he must have had leaving his former home ground on the winning side, a winning side that wasn't his former club. He forgot where he came from. He wouldn't have been there had we not given him the chance to have a breakdown.

The Mickey Bodley incident is only mentioned first to prepare you for the ULTIMATE betrayal. There has not been so despicable an incident since. The offender on this occasion was one Paul Culpin.

Cully was a strange one. There were times that he could play like an absolute dream, and times that he partnered Tony Adcock in such a way that they were an unbeatable combination. There were other times that he was so bad that the whole rest of the team couldn't carry him. I remember one game when, in front of the Hotel, the ball came down off the bar and all Cully had to do was nudge it a centimetre over the line with his head into an open goal. What happened is that Cully ducked under the ball and it rolled down his back. I'm sure that he'd forgotten which way he was playing, and that he was a striker, and sincerely believed that he was a defender heroically clearing the ball. As I remember, it got to a stage where he played too badly too often and he was shown the door... to P*sh. It seemed like a good thing for both of them. P*sh were gaining a poor Cobblers player, which put Cully worlds above the best that P*sh have ever had. From Cully's point of view, he was going to a club where a garden gnome is considered a footballing genius. From the Cobblers point of view, we were getting rid of Cully to P*sh, which couldn't be a bad thing... could it?

It was the same old story. Packed house for a local derby, it was a cert, we would win the game and the Nobel Peace Prize. That being the case it was only natural that the Cobblers should have an off day and P*sh won. But the nightmare went deeper, the scorer of the winning goal, the only goal to my memory, was Culpin. And there's more, I still shudder at the memory, he scored IN FRONT OF THE HOTEL!

The horror! I'm sure that everything that went wrong for the Cobblers after that was the result of that goal. Of course, Cully, no doubt to thank the Enders for their gracious welcome, celebrated TO the Hotel End. Its beggar's belief. Why would he do such a thing? He was very fortunate to only get a couple of Ansell burgers thrown at him and a few thousand Northamptonian expletives bellowed at him.

**Rambo... put it away**
One return to the club that will be remembered for all the right reasons was the visit of The Ducks' (Aylesbury), to the County Ground, which was notable also for the return of two other ex-Cobblers Graham 'Rambo' Reed and Glenville Donegal. The way I remember it, it was a good-natured affair for the fans of both sides and the teams. Glenville was asked to wave to the Hotel End and, while this was followed by, "Cobblers reject," even that did not feel malicious. Greater than either of these welcomes, however, was that given to Rambo. While the teams were lining up, Cobblers playing to the Hotel, Aylesbury from it, the cry went up, "Rambo, show us yer arse, Rambo, Rambo, show us yer arse." Rambo obliged. We close the page on that chapter.

**Other varied memories, including the chin**
We know that the declaration-of-the-opposition's-political-preferences song never caught on. Another guy never had his war-cry taken up but, fair play to him, week in, week out he'd give it his all. Every week, at least once during the game, we'd hear the familiar cry (solo every time), "Come on the Teyn, aaaggggh!" Not once did he get the, "On your own," song. No, this legend continued his solo career. So, to you sir, I say, "Well done."
We all know that Jimmy Hill never liked the Cobblers. He made that very clear every time we got a mention on his show. I had first-hand experience of his punditry-objectivity following one of our drubbings of the pre-Al Fayed Cottagers. I used to have the privilege on going into the members' bar as I knew the bar manager and my mum did the catering for the directors' bar. Anyway, following our boat-race day humiliation of Mohammed's future babies, I had just been let in by Gavin (legendary doorman) and was followed in by Mr Chin himself. Gavin asked the noted pundit his opinion on the game. Did the great expert put it down to a poor showing by his team? Was it due to a large number of injuries? Was the grass too long? None of the above. Apparently, the referee allowed the Hotel End to run the game. Now, seeing that Mr Hill was a great sage of the game, and noted as a pundit and therefore totally impartial, I think that the club owes everyone on the Hotel End that day a bonus payment.

I remember the chilling silence that came over the ground when the announcement of the events at Hillsborough.

When the Spion Kop became the away enclosure and some teams brought very few supporters. Singing, "You must have come in a taxi," was funny. It wasn't so amusing when we lost on such occasions.

The County Ground. Yes, it wasn't pretty. Yes, at the start of the season you still had to wait for the last cricket fan of the season to finish his cup of tea, put his picnic blanket in the boot and drive off before the game could start. But it had character, it had terracing, and sadly most modern grounds have neither.

**Norman Nickason**

# Chapter 3 - Metamorphosis

Ah the County Ground days! I can really relate to the memories in the previous chapter as they were my early Cobblers days. Even though we were relegated in the 1989/90 season, this somehow made my obsession even stronger. We were back in Division Four, but everyone knew we were going to win the league. Graham Carr had, sadly quit, but his exteam mate from the sixties, Theo Foley took charge. Ironically the first home league game of the season, Graham was back, this time with Blackpool. But a Bobby Barnes goal won the game for the Cobblers. The day was marred by the news that Ex-Cobbler Dave Longhurst had died during a game whilst playing for York City. There was a sombre atmosphere as fans left the ground, bringing a lump to a few throats.

**The footballing nation was shocked**

This was a little reminiscent of the blows that we all felt a couple of seasons before when we learnt of the Hillsborough disaster. We'd been beaten by Sheffield United at the County Ground and the announcement came over the tannoy. Of course, no mobile phones in those days meant that the news took a little while to filter through. The whole of the Hotel End simply froze as the words unfolded into our ears. I can remember that the away fans were still celebrating and didn't hear the story. As my mate Norman and I left the ground, we barely spoke and nobody else did either! Once outside, we were approached by Sheffield United fans who were trying to find out if the mumbled message they heard was true.

My mum had been out that day too and heard on the radio that football fans had lost their lives in a crush due to the big game. She didn't catch the whole story but heard Sheffield and panicked thinking that it had happened at the County Ground. Obviously at home, I realised her concern. She had been listening to Radio Northampton, caught the end of the story, knew there was a bigger crowd than expected at the County Ground and put two and two together. She was relieved to see me at home after the game I tell you. Obviously, this was a metamorphosis for the changing face of the game as we knew it, but not the main subject of this chapter. Moments like Hillsborough and Dave Longhurst really bring the football community down to earth with a bump. As much as we are obsessed as a nation, it proves that football isn't really life or death.

Back on the pitch, and the 29th September was quite a significant day at the County Ground. We played Halifax at home, it was the first game I went to with my best mate Justin, who wasn't really into the Cobblers. As the team was announced, it normally went, "In goal for the Cobblers, number one, Peter Gleasure..." cue the cheer from the crowd..."..number two..." and so on but today, it went, "..number one, Marlon Beresford..."

After over 300 consecutive appearances, Peter Gleasure was dropped from the starting line up. He didn't play a league game again until April. However, by December the anger at Gleasure being dropped by Foley had all but disappeared as a 3-2 win over Rochdale on December 1st meant my Saturday night pint was even sweeter. We were top of the league. I proudly wore my claret with a tine of pink zig-zag Cobblers shirt down town the Sunnyside pub that night. Sadly, two points from the last eight games turned us from promotion certs to tenth in the league and we never recovered!

**The romance of the FA Cup**

After the excitement of beating Coventry in 1990, we faced a few non-league teams over the following seasons. There was an enjoyable trip to Littlehampton in November 1990. I recall a bunch of home fans wearing marigold gloves in the crowd, their nickname was "The Marigolds."

The ground was like that of Northampton Spencer, with a small club house on one side. Of course, the town had gone football mad and everyone man and their rubber gloves came out to watch. Rows of temporary seats were erected around the perimeter. Town won 4-0 and it was all pretty easy, with the home side's cause not helped when their part time defender/part time window cleaner was sent off in the first half.

We faced Barnet in the next round and the first game was one of the coldest days in history. How the game wasn't snowed off, I don't know. We lost the replay and everyone hated Barnet.

The following season was a forgettable trip to Crawley and a 4-2 defeat. It all started to go to plan when Tony Adcock gave us the lead. I had gone to the game on the Mounties bus with a load of posties and one of my mates, Bob, needed a pee near the end of the first half. I was pretty bursting too, maybe a couple of extra pints too many had been sunk in the pub beforehand. We made our way through the shallow terrace to portaloos in the corner. Bob was more desperate than me, so I let him go first. As he was doing his business, Crawley equalised. Bob came running out of the portaloo moments later, cheering, only to realise that it was the home side who had scored. His face dropped as I shut the bog door behind me. As I came out, I looked straight towards the goal at the other end, only to see the ball fly into the net for 2-1 Crawley. We were both pretty gutted now, but by the time we had found our way back to our original spot, Phil Chard scrambled the ball home for an equaliser. Basically, three goals were scored in our trip to the toilet. The second half highlights included watching planes take off at Gatwick Airport as the Cobblers crashed out. Romance my ar*e!

**The match day experience**
Being a Cobblers fan at this point wasn't as much fun as I had experienced over my first couple of seasons, but match days were an enjoyable experience. If that makes any sense to you, you are doing well! Ok, I will explain; although the results were pretty poor on the pitch, a group of us now established our ritual. This involved meeting in the pub and we would enjoy a few pints before heading to the ground, sometimes enjoying a bag of chips along the way. Sound familiar? The journey of a regular fan from anywhere in the country. The beers would always help us get in the mood for the football that we were about to witness, as today, we would live in hope that we were going to start that winning run off. The Hotel End was sparsely populated nowadays, so a last-minute entrance through the Abington Avenue turnstiles was never a problem. It was tradition that we could never enter the ground through the Wantage Road turnstiles for two reasons. The first was that to us that was the cricket entrance and we were here to watch football, allegedly! The second reason; well it was bad luck of course! We must have been barking mad, wins came about as

regular as Christmas, but for some reason, we felt it bad luck not to go through the turnstiles on Abington Avenue.

Inside the ground, we would have no expectation of winning, so we would simply sing, have a laugh and take the Mickey out of everything and everyone around us. The spirit was great as most people joined in with the banter. We would invent songs and try and sing them and then celebrate like lunatics if we scored a consolation goal, or if the unthinkable happened and we actually won. We didn't care at this point.

**Trouble a brewing.**

Although there was an underlying problem that caught us unaware one day. Much has been written and talked about over the years about this era, but it was so significant, it has to be mentioned again. When someone takes over your football club, you believe that they do so with good intent. By the early nineties, the Premiership was already destined to go ahead and fans from the lower leagues feared the gulf widening. Northampton Town had enjoyed brief hope after running away with the Fourth Division title in 1986/87, but the new face in the hot seat was a certain Birmingham market trader Michael McRitchie whose name sends shudders down the spines of many Cobblers fans. He came on board when the club hadn't got two pennies to rub together and he left the club in a situation where hard cash would not have solved the credit problems. Quite why a second hand crockery trader wanted with a struggling Fourth Division club was beyond anyone.

Newport County dropped out of the league a few seasons earlier, then went out of business completely. Nobody really seemed to care! Maidstone United, who sold their ground and bought their way into the football league, soon followed suit. I remember going there once, well to the home of Dartford which they shared. The facilities were awful, nowhere good enough for league football. Although Maidstone shot themselves through the heart, they also went out of business. Next Aldershot and Northampton were reported to be on the verge. I am not sure what made me most angry about the situation, the fact that we had a clueless chairman who seemed intent on killing the club or the fact that the then Chief Executive of Manchester United implying that clubs at the top needed more clubs like ours to go out of business. It was classed as natural wastage and supposedly good for the sport.

But our little group continued to go home and away to support the team. The off the pitch problems made us feel closer knit to the club, especially the players who were giving it their all for the shirt. At the end of the 1991/92 season, we scored nine goals between February and the end of the season. A total of seventeen games. Luckily earlier results had been just good enough to keep us in the football league.

Our goal count in the baron run that followed, would have been higher if it wasn't for the demise of Aldershot. Talking to my old mate Bob Duff, we reminisced about a great win that never technically happened. We ended up losing six points as a result of the Shots demise, but I'll let Bob take you through the story of this day out at the Recreation Ground...

# The Game That Never Was...In North Hants!

I used to be a regular at the County Ground in the 80's and 90's but a part of me died when the Cobblers moved to Sixfields. I missed the good old days standing on the Hotel End with my mates. We hadn't a care in the world and on the pitch, things were never great, but the main order of the day was a few beers, a social chat and a sing song on the terraces.

One day that will always stick in my mind was 7th March 1992 and six of us had decided to make a rare car journey to an away game. Normally we would go on the Mounties bus, but today, we decided to convey to Aldershot with two designated drivers. Ok, two cars weren't much of a convoy, but I drove my claret Ford Escort and my mate Mark (the producer of this fine book) took his beige Ford Fiesta. The convoy broke up as we lost each other in Abington and the next time we met up was in the away end at Aldershot.

A crowd of about 2,500 turned up to watch could be the last ever meeting of both sides, The Cobblers were going through some scary times with the threat of winding up orders over unpaid bills thanks to our chairman Michael McRitchie. Aldershot were actually in a worse position than us, they were about two weeks from going completely out of business and were leading that unwanted race.

There was a sombre atmosphere around the ground as we arrived just as the teams were about to kick off. Our other half of the convoy were already standing on the away terrace, so we made our way around the pitch and joined the few hundred Cobblers fans in the corner.

Both sets of supporters began chanting "Sack the board, sack the board, sack the board" at their respective owners. We were angry at the situation our clubs had been allowed to get into, but full of passion.

**A stunning 25 yard shot lobbed Barry Richardson**

The home side took the lead on about 25 minutes with a stunning 25-yard shot which lobbed Cobblers' keeper Barry 'Psycho' Richardson. The home fans started to jeer us a little, but we continued chanting and singing. More sack the board chants rung out before the home fans starting singing "Northampton, Northampton, Northampton." We were in a state of shock for a moment and the away end went quiet. In the midst of the silence, our group of six suddenly bust into a rendition of "Aldershot, Aldershot, Aldershot" towards the home end.

A few other Cobblers fans joined in this moment of unity between two sets of troubled supporters, before somebody walked over to us and informed us that the Shots' fans were actually singing "North Hants Shire" not the name of our town. At this point, we were past caring and continued the bond between the fans. The Shots' faithful were a little reluctant at first but then bust into a chorus of "McRitchie Out" which got a massive cheer.

Just before half time, we equalised through Christian Edwards, so it was 1-1 at half time. During the break, we decided to amuse ourselves with a game of Mexican Hat! If you've never played this before, it basically involves nicking someone's hat and passing it around the heads of as many people in the crowd. The hat went around the away end before Mark through it over the fence into the home end. An Aldershot fan put it on his head and 'Mexican Hat' continued. That proved to be part two in the bond as the Shots' fans began chatting to us through the fence and soon a joint protest against both clubs' owners were discussed. After some gentle discussions with the stewards, some of the home faithful joined us in the away end. No sooner had we shook hands, Aidy Thorpe put the Cobblers in front and we found ourselves jumping around, going balmy with ten home fans joining in.

**It was fruitless**

More Aldershot fans joined us in the away end until there was probably about fifty or so. We chanted in anger at the boards and sang each other's team's songs. Another goal from Dean Edwards and a fourth from Christian McClean made it 4-1 to the Cobblers, but our new friends joined in our celebrations. They were all fruitless, as Aldershot went bust weeks later and the 4-1 victory was wiped from all records.

In an age of fans unity days where fans from all over the country get together to support a club in trouble, I can't help feeling that we must have been the first club to be a part of fans unity. It's fitting to see the Shots regain their league status sixteen years later.

**Survival**

Aldershot only lasted a few more weeks before they were wound up and they resigned from the league, with all their results being wiped from the records. I was devastated as I heard the news. For a start, 4-1 away wins didn't happen very often anymore, but more to the point, these Shots fans that we had met weeks before now didn't have a club to support. Hearing about multi-million-pound player sales on the television were pretty hard to stomach now, as the next few weeks were about survival. There seemed to be very little sympathy from the rest of the footballing world, as the impression was almost "good riddance."

**The Lincoln Weekend.**

A couple of weeks later, Bob and I had a great weekend planned, which centred around drinking and a trip to Lincoln. We decided to get the train to Sincil Bank instead of the usual trip on the bus, this would mean more drinking en-route. I got cheap train tickets as Boots were doing a two for one offer, this coupled with a Young Person's Railcard discount meant we had a few more beer tokens to spend on the trip. I am sure that we left Northampton station still p*ssed from the night before. The train took so long to get to Lincoln that we never actually got a chance to go to the pub, so we made do with tins of lager all the way.

There was a good turnout of Cobblers fans on the terrace at the side of the pitch and we were soon cheering as Mickey Bell curled in a beauty from the corner of the area before Stuart Beavon scored a second from the spot. The game ended 2-1, so we headed to the city centre to celebrate, but no pubs would let us in as we had colours on. We had to make do with Threshers for some celebratory liquid refreshments, but soon realised that we had bought Carlsberg, the boycotted lager. They had decided to pull out of sponsoring the Cobblers and go to Anfield instead. It was a tossup between chucking the remaining six cans in the river or accepting that the brewery already had our money and drinking them to spite them. We chose the latter.

Although we were trying to make the best of the situation, we were hit with a low blow a couple of weeks later...

**Story Inspired by Bob Duff**

# A New Beginning of Uncertainty

On 4th April 1992 Northampton Town ran out at Underhill, Barnet with a handful of youth teamers in the starting line up, the day after the club had gone into administration. The previous day, the administrators Kerr Pannell and Foster moved into the County Ground releasing the following players;

Christian McLean, Irvin Gernon, Aidy Thorpe, Greg Campbell, Trevor Quow, Dave Johnson, Peter Gleasure, Scott Stackman, Lee Colkin and David Scope. Manager Theo Foley and his assistant Joe Kiernan were also given their P45s in a move that shocked the town.

I remember walking in the front door and being greeted with this news from my mum. Mum isn't a football fan, so at first, I doubted the accuracy of the story, saying that a club doesn't just sack their players. I also thought she was winding me up because we'd been playing poorly of late. But she remained serious and switched on Anglia News to confirm the truth in the matter. I can't remember what I felt at the time, I just got ready and headed down the pub to talk to my mates about the situation.

**Whatever happened I was going to Barnet the next day**

A few hours later, the news started to sink in. As the evening unfolded, the Cobblers supporting few in our group began to feel delighted that the Chairman Michael McRitchie had gone. We were pleased that all the protests at the previous games had made a point and appeared to have worked. But on the other hand, we were scared. Scared of the situation that swallowed Aldershot and Newport County only a year or so earlier. But whatever happened, we were going to Barnet the next day. Everyone non-Cobblers thought we were mad; they just didn't see the point. But we had a duty! We may not have a club to watch next season, so now was the time to make the most of it.

**Everyone was still looking forward to the game**

The following day was normal at first, heading into Town to catch the Mounties bus to North London. The mood on board was surprisingly buoyant as everyone was really looking forward to the game, despite what looked to be an inevitable defeat.

**Toothpaste was missing**

On the bus we compared that starting line up from the 2-2 home draw with Rochdale on the 31st March, which was only four days earlier. Christian McClean, fondly remembered as 'Toothpaste' scored both the Cobblers goals on the night, but he wouldn't be scoring today, he was no longer a Cobblers player.

After a couple of pints in the pub, we wandered along the lane behind the Underhill ground and behind the away terrace. Suddenly one of my mates bellowed out "Phil Chard's Claret Army!" Seconds later, the same chant was heard from inside the ground and the singing in the away end didn't stop until we got back on the bus at 5pm.

A crowd of 2,816 witnessed the home side win 3-0, the 1,000 or so Cobblers fans in attendance barely noticed the goals hit the net. We were totally blinkered to the jibes from the home ends; all we cared about was that we still had a club to support.

At the final whistle, new player manager Phil Chard and assistant player manager Stuart Beavon brought the players over the travelling fans and paraded around as if they'd just won the FA Cup. Some of the younger players had tears in their eyes, as did many of those watching on the terraces.

For anyone who was at Underhill on the day, they will probably remember this as a new beginning for Northampton Town Football Club.

The players who continued on the books at County Ground, played out the rest of the season with big hearts. Nobody in that squad would be playing for a big fat pay cheque at the end of the month, it was purely personal pride.

Nowadays I still find it hard to talk to fans of Premiership clubs who tell me how desperate they are for a new striker to add to their five or six existing forwards in the squad. My mind always goes back to Barnet for a while and put things into perspective. For anyone interested, here are the starting line ups from that week in 1992;

**Tuesday 31st March 1992 - Northampton Town 2-2 Rochdale**
Barry Richardson, Mark Parsons, Steve Terry, Aidy Thorpe, Terry Angus, Jason Burnham, Stuart Beavon, Micky Bell, Irving Gernon, Steve Brown,

Christian McLean (subs) Greg Campbell and Danny Kiernan. Manager Theo Foley, Assistant Manager Joe Kiernan

**Saturday 4th April 1992 - Barnet 3-0 Northampton Town**

Barry Richardson, Mark Parsons, Steve Terry, Sean Parker, Terry Angus, Jason Burnham, Stuart Beavon, Micky Bell, Danny Kiernan, Steve Brown, Phil Chard. (subs): Martin Aldridge, Ricky Bulzis. Manager Phil Chard, Assistant Manager, Stuart Beavon

As you can see, the team didn't change a lot, but included graduates from the youth team like Danny Kiernan and Ricky Bulzis who were now full-time players. Northampton Town Football Club managed to play their further five fixtures and completed the season with a 2-1 victory at Hereford, but many fans wondered "what would the future hold?"

*An optimistic message at the County Ground during hard times. (Mark White)*

# Barnet

It's quite funny, but whilst putting this book together, I have been contacted by quite a few Barnet fans to offer their opinions. Back in the nineties, many Cobblers fans hated this club with a passion. A handful rivalled them to P*sh at times, although they could never touch that history and rivalry. I'll be honest, I wasn't too fond of the Bees myself, I didn't like the ground, the fans and the manager, Barry Fry of course.

As time has passed, I've grown to respect them a little more and this has certainly been helped by these fans who got in contact in recent times.

**What a week**

I suppose the side from Underhill have never really had a dull moment since our paths first crossed in 1990. When they finally won the Conference and were promoted, Barnet lost their 1st league game 7-4 at home to Lincoln before drawing 5-5 with Brentford in the League Cup in their league debut week and it has been a rollercoaster since then. They certainly hold Northampton with a bit of respect even though we were classed loosely as their derby rivals for a while.

**#Sixfields is a great stadium, the County Ground was fascinating**

Bees fan Jonathan said "I have always quite liked Northampton for a number of reasons such as the fascination with the old County Ground. I also went to see the Third Division Play Off final v Swansea. My dad and I didn't have a ticket and we couldn't buy tickets on the day; a Northampton fan had a couple of spare tickets next to us and he let us buy them at face value, he could have sold them at a profit to a tout but chose not to. Although the game was very dull the celebrations in the ground afterwards were excellent."

Jonathan also added "Although I don't care much about Northampton. I really enjoyed my visit to Sixfields a couple of seasons back, especially because we won. It's a great ground. I've been to Northampton twice with Barnet, the first time I was still very young and we got beaten. The second time was when the Bees staged a memorable comeback and won 2-1 late on. I've never found any problems with Northampton fans, players or the Sixfields Stadium. Funnily enough, I used to have quite a soft spot for the

Cobblers, as I saw them win in the Wembley play-off final in 1997 against Swansea. Nothing against them, seem a friendly club."

In fact, whilst we're on the subject of Barnet, I was sent a great story about a fan who actually got to play for his team. The story briefly goes...

It must be every football fans dream to run out onto the pitch in their clubs' colours and play for their team. It can't happen very often but for Barnet superfan Steve Percy that dream came true on Tuesday the 2nd December 2003 when Barnet played Ware in the Herts Senior Cup. Steve won a prize draw to play for the first team and was brought on with about five minutes to go with the Bees winning 4-1. Manager Martin Allen told him to hang in the centre circle. The Ware players were a little unhappy with a fan being involved in the match and showed their gratitude by taking Steve out within a minute. Here is his account of what happened; "I'd been on for a minute or so and saw the ball coming towards me and managed to get a reasonable touch on it, flicking it off to a Barnet player. The next thing I know someone's come through the back of me, it was a really bad tackle and took me straight out. He should have been sent off but the referee booked him, but prior to that other Ware players had come over pushing and shoving, which resulted in a Ware player getting his second yellow and sent off."

So within a minute of realising your boyhood dream of playing for your side, there is a mass brawl going on around you and the players you watch week in week out are sticking up for you. Great stuff...

**We made it**

Anyway, enough about Barnet for now, although I have a feeling that we will hear more about them later. Post McRitchie, there was a sense of relief as we kicked off the following season at Gillingham, but the off the pitch troubles were far from over. Transfer embargos and debts threatened, but the supporters were having an input with the newly formed supporters trust. A last-minute winner from player-manager Phil Chard at The Priestfield Stadium sent Cobblers fans delirious on day one, but wins didn't exactly flow after that. In reality, the opening day win gave us all false hope as bigger problems were around the corner. The off-pitch problems were really taking their toll and the damage had been done. As fans, we tried our best to keep ourselves entertained on the terraces though, relishing every rare win and every goal scored.

## Christmas party

The 1992/93 cup run was a different matter though, as reaching the third round was as much as an achievement as winning the cup. Ok, that was an exaggeration, but a 3-1 first round win over Fulham lifted everyone's spirits, before we were struck with fear at the second round draw. Bath City away! We spoke of our non-league team record a couple of pages ago. The part timers held us to a 2-2 draw in the first game and forced a replay at the County Ground.

I recall this night as it was my work's team Christmas party. It was a difficult situation because our team had some money in a pot and paid some towards our meal. There was no way I was going to miss the football, so I decided to make a late entrance at the meal (much to work's disgust). I stuck on a smart shirt and trousers and made my way, very overdressed, to the County Ground. Midway through the second half it was still goal less and I was starting to imagine the wrath of my colleagues if the game went to extra time. Thankfully Mickey Bell broke the deadlock with a cute finish in front of the Hotel End. We went mad, it was a great goal celebration and everyone surged forward. The only problem was the big gap in the middle of the terrace as the surging crowd met thin air. I ended up on the floor underneath a pile of people. It ended 3-0 and a home tie with Rotherham awaited us in the third round.

I ran home, hopped in the car and bombed up the Wellingborough Road to join the Christmas meal. Upon arrival, the main course was just being served up and my starter was still waiting. I noticed a few funny looks from my work mates before realising I had dust and dirt all over my trousers and shirt from the goal celebration. It was worth it! We eventually went out to Rotherham in the next round thanks to a sickening last-minute goal and would've faced Newcastle at home in the next round, which made it even more devastating for me. I will explain soon.

## Nail biter

The season ended with a massive nail biter. Things really started to hit home as we all started to feel that the last home game of the season against Wrexham could have been the last ever league game to be played at the County Ground. The visitors won 2-0 to secure promotion and thousands of fans from North Wales invaded the pitch. It was sickening and to make matters worse, we had to wait another ten days for the crucial last match of the season at Shrewsbury. It seems completely pointless me telling you the story of what happened on the day of 8th May 1993, as many will have heard it many times before.

We all remember the feeling of doom as the half time whistle sounded and the home side lead 2-0. Their fans were celebrating a play-off spot and we were staring Conference football in the face. The saving grace was that Halifax were not winning. The celebration when Phil Chard pounced on a poor back pass to pull a goal back was good, but I can still see Pat Gavin's equaliser hitting the roof of the net. The goal celebration seemed to go on forever. Hereford scored and the celebration of that news seemed to blend in to the one of the equaliser. Who would have thought that one man's rear end would be the most loved rear end in Northampton from that day onwards? The feeling of sheer emotion as the ball hit Gavin on the arse before hitting the back of the net was one that still gives any Cobblers fan in attendance huge goose bumps. This was better than winning the FA Cup or any European competition.

**Fog on the Tyne**
Following the game, I headed north to visit my girlfriend of the time, who lived in Newcastle. Although I missed the celebrations with my mates, I chatted with many fans of other clubs on the train. Some of the Bury fans who had been sitting in the seats above the away terrace bought me a beer, as our win meant that they made the play offs instead of Shrewsbury. Ironically, they were without a game that day and were there to join in the celebrations. More ironically, the beer they bought me from the buffet car was the boycotted Carlsberg. Never mind, I couldn't be rude and not drink it. An Everton fan and a group of Sunderland fans were also very congratulatory on the way, plus generous with their beers. I finally arrived in Newcastle sporting my Cobblers scarf and a huge grin as wide as the River Tyne.

This was to be my last game as a Northampton resident as I moved to Newcastle that summer and became a Cobbler in exile. Whilst I left home, the Cobblers were also to move home very soon afterwards...

# The Home of the Cobblers

**A unique three-sided football arena**

My early years of following the Cobblers were at the dilapidated County Ground - that unique three-sided football arena. I have stood on the terrace next to the 'Meccano Stand', stood on the Spion Kop, stood on the Cricket Side and stood on the infamous Hotel End as well as one appearance in a temporary stand next to the Spion Kop. I can't really remember the old wooden stand that ran the length of Abington Avenue, although have obviously seen many photos of it. With that stand in place the ground didn't look too bad, but with the *'Meccano stand'*, complete with its 350 seats, it was only a matter of time before we had to move on. Sadly, the move took too long. Various proposals never got very far but in 1994 Sixfields was built. I enjoyed the atmosphere in the Hotel End during the final few years at the County Ground. That was where thousands of fans would gather to sing and cheer their heroes on. I was happy and proud to be a part of that. Some of my favourite County Ground memories include the all-conquering Fourth Division title winning side of 1986/87. As mentioned, that was my first season as a regular and we saw only one defeat and scored loads, 56 goals as many a team were swept aside by the likes of Richard Hill, Trevor Morley, Ian Benjamin, Eddie McGoldrick and all. Who knows what we might have achieved if we hadn't sold them all!? Even when some of those players weren't available though, we still managed a goal or five. I remember beating a very poor Rochdale that season 5-0 with loan man Paul McMenemy, son of Lawrie bagging a brace. It was a tremendous season, which we have yet to better.

**A Marco Van Basten like volley in front of the Spion Kop**

My favourite goal at the County Ground was the following season against Fulham. We needed a win to give us a chance of a play-off place. My Uncle Steve had got us passes for the player's bar that day also. It was Paul Culpin who scored the crucial goal in a 3-2 win. It was a first-time volley, from a tight angle, Marco Van Basten-like at the Spion Kop end. Fulham's keeper was big Jim Stannard who dropped a Dave Gilbert cross into the net for one of the other goals. My dad bought Culpin a pint after the game. The players in those days seemed to like a good drink.

The biggest one-off game I saw at the County Ground was probably the one against Coventry City in the FA Cup in 1990. It was a very wet day and I was stood on the Cricket Side with my dad, getting very wet. Coventry were a regular top-flight side in those days and three years earlier had won the cup of course. Steve Berry slid in and converted Bobby Barnes' cross in the 42nd minute to score the only goal of the game. It was a great performance and even better result. I bought four or five of the Sunday papers the following day just to read the reports from that day. The Independent stated that the Cobblers were a very talented side. I was obviously very proud to read that as it has stuck with me all this time! We also made the main news on BBC One that evening. I recorded that and the local coverage of the game as well as buying the official club video! Well, you can never have too much Cobblers, can you?

*The familiar view from the Hotel End. The floodlights dominate the background towering over the Spion Kop Terrace which only reached the centre of the pitch. The gap behind the goal on the right-hand side is home to the bowls club.*

I was a big fan of Tony Adcock, the flame-haired striker who scored a lot of goals and Bobby Barnes who would run at defences at will and also scored a good number of goals. Inexplicably Michael McRitchie sold them to the old enemy at London Road for next to nothing. The McRitchie era was depressing. He came in with claims of being a rich man to turn the club around again. All he achieved was taking us to the brink of extinction. I remember the red card McRitchie Out protest and also going to court to witness the winding-up order served on the club. Thankfully we got a reprieve and a few weeks later McRitchie finally left and we went into administration. That day in 1992 when nine players, manager Theo Foley and assistant Joe Kiernan were sacked was one of the saddest days following the Cobblers. The next day we travelled to Barnet with a scratch side and lost 3-0. The result didn't matter one bit. The thousand or so Cobblers fans that travelled were just pleased to still have a side to watch. We sang all game and the players ran over to us at the final whistle to hug us and shake hands and thank us for our support. I think they were as proud to have us as fans as we were to have them as players.

As ever with the Cobblers things are not straightforward. The much-billed last ever game at the County Ground against Chester City on April 30th 1994 wasn't actually the last ever game there. Because Sixfields wasn't going to be ready in time for the start of the 1994/95 season we had to play four more games at the County Ground. It was a shame really because the Chester game was a great occasion. 6,500 packed in to see a 1-0 win with Kevin Wilkin scoring the only goal with a 30 yard scorcher in the first minute. The actual final game at the County Ground was a tame affair against Mansfield that we lost 1-0 in front of just 4,993. Cobblers legends Ray Warbuton, Ian Samspon and Neil Grayson all played that night, players that went on to have great careers at the new home of football – Sixfields.

**Sitting there, we thought we were at the San Siro**
The first day against Barnet was a landmark occasion. After years of struggle at a crumbling old County Ground, a bright new era was dawning. A lovely sunny day greeted us as we made our way to this shiny new stadium. I thought the capacity of 7,600 was a little on the small side but after spending the previous four or five years struggling and averaging 3,500 it was more than adequate and the facilities were a big step up from the County Ground. I sat on the front row of the North Stand for this game with Barry, Matty and a few of the other lads that I regularly watched the Cobblers with in those days. Sitting there we thought we were at the San

Siro after being used to the County Ground! The match started off in typically nervy fashion with not too many clear-cut chances. The second half however was better and the Cobblers carved out numerous goalscoring chances. I think we hit the woodwork three times before the late Martin Aldridge scored a wonder goal to send the home support into raptures. His back-flip celebration was fitting to the occasion. In the melee after the goal my glasses flew off and were later handed back to me in a state of disrepair! Unfortunately, we couldn't hold on for the win as Dougie Freedman scored the equaliser.

The first win at Sixfields though came one week later against Wigan. Neil Grayson bagging the winner in the damp conditions. We thought that would be the turning point but things are never that simple. We had an average side managed by John Barnwell and results took a downturn and he was eventually sacked, to be replaced by a certain Ian Atkins. It was Atkins that was to give the Cobblers some steel and fighting spirit. He moulded together a very committed side, made up hardworking players and everything began to click. This culminated with the play-off success in the centenary year of 1997. The semi-final second leg against Cardiff was the first real pressure-cooker atmosphere at the new stadium. A 1-0 first leg win gave us the edge but with the controversial Uriah Rennie the man in the middle anything could happen. We needn't have worried as we won 3-2 and our old friend Rennie sending off Cardiff's Jeff Eckhart. The scenes at the final whistle were amazing. The Cobblers, who had struggled along for the past eight or nine years were at Wembley for the first time ever.

**He was hardly a free kick specialist**

I queued up for hours for my final ticket on Cup Final day and looked forward to the day. The sight of 32,000 Cobblers fans inside Wembley really was a sight to behold. A good atmosphere was created and we hoped for the best! In truth the game itself was poor with not too many chances and as we reached the 90th minute, extra-time seemed inevitable. That was before Mr John Frain took a free-kick. Hardly a free-kick specialist we hoped for the best. The kick was charged down illegally and the referee ordered a re-take. The rest as they say is history. I grabbed my camera, as I, and most of the other Cobblers fans seemed to know what was going to happen. And yes, it did. John Frain curled the ball around the wall and into the left-hand corner of the net. GOAL!! 1-0. The Cobblers fans went wild. I have a great photo of the ball about to go in. Swansea kicked off – Jan Molby shooting from the kick-off as the referee blew for full-time. Then the party began and the club adopted *Simply The Best* as the new anthem (for the time-being at least). Unforgettable scenes. Thank you John Frain.

The open-top bus tour of the town on the following Bank Holiday Monday saw thousands upon thousands of Cobblers fans line the town's streets to greet their heroes. The town had never seen anything like it before.

Atkins continued to work miracles the following season with plenty of home wins as well as picking up some useful results on the road. Fulham were spending big that season but we took four points off of them. We also secured a great point at Watford's Vicarage Road, Dean Peer netting a late equaliser. Against the odds another play-off spot was secured. The first leg of the semi-final at Bristol Rovers was nothing short of a disaster, until big John Gayle scored a late but crucial goal. This meant 'only' a two-goal deficit. The feeling outside and inside Sixfields for the second leg was one I'd never experienced before. Everyone sensed victory and everyone played their part. I had the good fortune of winning a Chronicle & Echo competition to present Dean Peer with the Player of the Month award on the pitch before the game. This also meant I got player's lounge passes. The atmosphere was the best ever. You could smell the excitement, the tension, and the expectation. Everyone was up for it. The game was also non-stop. Every time the ball went out of play the ball-boys were quick to retrieve it to get play re-started as soon as possible. Carl Heggs made the crucial breakthrough in the first half. He then turned his man beautifully to set up Ian Clarkson for the second. Rovers were never in it and the Cobblers wanted another. We got another one too from Ray Warburton. It was the stuff of dreams. If you were writing a script, that would have been it. The final whistle went which was the cue for much pandemonium. Rovers fans were silent, in total disbelief at what they had just witnessed. We partied and celebrated another Wembley appearance!

A phenomenal 42,000 Cobblers fans packed into Wembley for the final against Grimsby. Sadly, we witnessed another poor game and lost 1-0. I suppose the highlight was Woody's penalty save. Despite the defeat many thousands of Cobblers fans stayed behind cheering the team, drowning out the minimal noise from the 12,000 Grimsby fans.

We have always flirted between the Third and Fourth tiers of English football and have had three promotions and so far, two relegations since being at Sixfields, so life is rarely dull. We have also had some great cup wins including the humbling of West Ham in the League Cup. The worst time was the ill-fated Terry Fenwick era. Although only here for seven games it was a very unpleasant time. Thankfully David Cardoza saw sense and we have improved ever since. Promotion under Calderwood perhaps took a season or two too long but he brought a very professional approach to the club. I actually worked at the club on match days as a host in the corporate hospitality areas during the 2003/04 season. It was a great insight into the hard work that goes on behind the scenes. Most of us never get to see that. For me it was an honour to be associated with the club and I enjoyed meeting the corporate guests and sponsors. Being the Cobblers I was never going to meet too many famous faces but Graham Souness, Peter Taylor, Stuart Pearce, Jo Whiley and Barry Fry all came through the Sixfields doors! And of course, we played Manchester United in the FA Cup. Unfortunately for me I was posted at Franklins Gardens looking after 200 guests there before being bussed up to Sixfields!

What is really important now that we have established ourselves in League One is that we do not slip back into the basement division. We have an excellent manager who is building a good young side and the future looks bright. However, it is the stadium that could hold us back. When built it was fit for its purpose of housing a struggling basement side but now, unless we get the go ahead for re-development, we may never get to reach the promised land of the Championship. The Town is big enough and there is enough support out there to fill an expanded stadium and I hope that one day in the not too distant future this will be the case. Whatever happens however, I will always be a Cobblers supporter. It's easy to start supporting a Prem club from your armchair but following the highs and many lows of a lower league club takes real commitment. I, for one am proud to be a Cobbler.

**Lee Wade**

# Chapter 4 - Hit the Road

The general consensus across the world of football is that fans enjoy away trips more than they do home games. And why not? The appeal of going to a place that you wouldn't normally go to. There is also the appeal of a smaller, close knit group of fans to meet up with on the road. It is almost a quest or an adventure of sorts.

**Love it**

Personally, I always love a trip to Rochdale. Rarely do we win there, but it's friendly atmosphere, the pub right next to the ground, a chippy just across the road, it all has a traditional feel to it. Bournemouth is also a favourite. A trip to the seaside, a rare chance to go to a match with my dad (he lives there remember), it is always a weekend away. However, we never win there either. For results, Macclesfield's Moss Rose is great for an away day. Marc Richards scoring four first half goals in a 4-0 win in 2004, plus he had one disallowed as well. That was the pick of the bunch!

**Urgh**

On the other side of the coin, there are some less desirable away trips such as Luton. A local derby, but an awful ground and we have terrible form there. Swansea is a terrible journey and Colchester seems to take forever to get to. Although now they have said goodbye to Layer Road, that must lighten the appeal for some travelling fans. Of course, many clubs have left their spiritual homes now.

**Singing a little song**

Singing always seems better away from home too. One of the most pointless chants I ever remember was at Port Vale in 1993. We had reached the quarter finals of the then Auto Windscreens Shield.

The home side were favourites to win but we were hopeful of an upset at 2-2. Vale scored a couple of late goals to make it 4-2. In the final minutes, a couple of Vale fans in the opposite end held a small flag above their heads. At that point, the abundance of flags in the away end was displayed in a similar fashion accompanied with the chant "What's it like to be out-flagged." This went on for the remainder of the game. Why Vale would have been bothered about being "out-flagged" is beyond me, but it made us all laugh.

**P*ss on your party**

I always feel indebted to the three Everton fans who helped my mate Steve and witness a great Cobblers moment. Our road trip that day in April 1997 was to Craven Cottage, hoping for a result to take us a step closer to the play offs. Already promoted Fulham needed a win to clinch the league title. We drove down to Golders Green and picked up the tube to Putney Bridge. Thinking that we'd see the floodlights from the train, we became increasingly worried that kick off was nearing, but a Fulham fan on the tube told us it was "a bit of a walk" to the ground. We started sprinting in the general direction of Craven Cottage when a car pulled up alongside us and the passenger offered us a lift to the game. Those things that my mum told me about getting into a strangers' car went out of the window as it was now 3pm. We learnt that these lads were Evertonians and were on their way to their Sunday clash at Southampton, so they decided to take in a big London game (which of course was Fulham v Northampton). They dropped us right outside the away end and told us to get inside and support our team. The minute we walked onto the terrace, we looked up to see Jason White break clear from the halfway line, round the keeper and score for 1-0. It was a glorious moment and we were so grateful to three scousers who made it possible for us to witness. Thank you! Of course, that goal was good enough to delay Fulham's promotion party for another week too.

**Missing**

One away trip that I was always gutted to have missed was the trip to Deepdale the year before when Neil Grayson's hat-trick stunned the Champions. I had planned to go, but after a heavy night out I woke up at two in the afternoon. Rarely do I sleep in that much.

Cambridge used to annoy me only because I would always get lost on the way to the Abbey Stadium, it took six attempts to see a kick off there.

Whatever made me travel to Carlisle in 1992 was beyond me. An inevitable depressing 2-0 defeat and then you have over 250 miles to get home. I went with Lee Wade that day, he mentions it in a couple of pages. The Mounties had a minibus and it was very quiet on the way home.

Of all the places that I have been, Cardiff and Millwall have always been the most intimidating. We always remember the play off semi at Ninian Park. I have vowed not to go there again, which is a shame for the genuine supporters of Cardiff City. Having to run for the supporters' bus was not a great way to end a fantastic game. I stupidly parked near the home end at Millwall once. After visiting the previous season and not experiencing any problems, I didn't give it a second thought. On the way back to the car, I feared for my life as I was found out not to be a home fan. They saw some claret shirt protruding out of the bottom of my coat.

On the flip side, I have enjoyed drinks with fans of Rochdale, Bury, Mansfield, Oxford, Barnet, Darlington, Grimsby, Leyton Orient, Notts County, Tranmere and Swansea on my travels. The banter and wind up inside the ground is always part and parcel of the fun of football, but at the end of the day, we all support our club for the same reason. And that is to feel part of it.

So let's take a short trip around the country and hear from a few Cobblers and their experiences on the road...

# Away Days

**An ideal first away trip**

Season 1987/88 saw me make my first away trip. It was the opening day of this season and the venue was Sealand Road, home of Chester City. I went with my Uncle Steve, another life-long Cobbler and a couple of his mates. I was very young and impressionable but Uncle Steve is a perfect role model! What a game. For a first away game it doesn't get any better. We won 5-0 with five different goal scorers. Sadly, subsequent away trips have never been as successful. In total by the end of the 2007/08 season I have seen the Cobblers on their travels eighty-three times. Of those games only seventeen have been won. That's a poor record, although it is probably blighted by the fact that I made most of my away trips during the dark days of the early nineties before I was married and had children. Following your side away from home is a sign of true commitment and you do feel like a diehard fan, especially at grim places like Maidstone, Scarborough or Halifax. And for me, witnessing a Cobblers away win is a rare and precious commodity.

**You came all this way, just to lose**

Of the lowlights I think the FA Cup tie at Rochdale in 1990 ranks as one of the worst. Having seen off Coventry in the third round, a trip to Spotland seemed a formality. After all they were in a league below us and were, as usual, having a poor season. What followed was totally unexpected and a massive disappointment. Town never got going and Rochdale deserved their 3-0 victory and a place in the fifth round. I remember getting caught in a snowstorm on the way home too. Crawley Town also in the FA Cup, in 1991 was a disaster. We managed to lose 4-2 in a terrible performance. I have actually only seen the Cobblers win one FA Cup tie away from home and that was at Kettering in 1989 when Dean Thomas scored the winner from about 40 yards. Match Of The Day showed highlights that evening which was the first time I had ever seen the Cobblers on MOTD. Of the other low points (there are too many to write about), losing 7-0 at Scunthorpe in 1993 is high on the list. We had beaten Mansfield 5-1 on the previous Tuesday, so we travelled to Glanford Park in good spirits. Unfortunately, we were played off the park and the unfortunate Steve

Sherwood had to pick the ball out of the net SEVEN times. Despite this I travelled to Walsall on the following Tuesday night for an Autoglass Trophy game (I obviously had too much time and spare money in those days). Barry "Psycho" Richardson was recalled in goal and we managed a 0-0 draw.

I have travelled to the far-flung places like Carlisle (lost 2-0 in 1992). We travelled up on a mini-bus that had one passenger too many who had to sit on the floor all the way there, and back! I've seen us lose 2-0 at Torquay on a wet Tuesday night, draw 0-0 at Exeter and lose 3-1 at Darlington's old Feethams ground where I tasted my first pint of Tetleys bitter. I have made the trip to Lincoln City's home, Sincil Bank, nine times and have still not seen a win. I think we have won there once while I have been a Cobblers fan and I missed it! The 4-3 defeat under John Barnwell was exciting in 1993, but the 3-2 defeat under Colin Calderwood in 2004 was depressing. We were 2-0 up at half-time and I thought I had broken the hoodoo at the ninth time of asking. It was not meant to be though. Unbelievably we fell apart in the 2nd half and lost 3-2 to a last-minute goal. I was gutted, again!

It hasn't all been doom and gloom on my travels though. One of the obscure highlights was the 4-1 win at Aldershot in 1992. It was the season that a certain Michael McRitchie (a name I hate writing or saying) took us to the brink of extinction. It was also the season where Aldershot went beyond the brink and folded before the end of the season. Because of both club's predicaments there was good banter and plenty of harmony between both sets of fans. So much so that the stewards opened up the gates dividing the fans so we could chat and share our woes together. I swapped scarves with an Aldershot fan and I still have that scarf today. The result that day wasn't important. As it turned out, it never stood as sadly Aldershot were wound up, so all of the results against them were expunged. A shame for Dean Edwards as he scored twice that day – his only goals for the Cobblers but alas they don't count, therefore, technically, he never did score for the Cobblers!

**At the final whistle we clambered over the fence**

One of the most nervous trips though was Shrewsbury, May 8th 1993. Our Football League future depended on us winning this game. Shrewsbury were going for the play-offs so it was a hugely difficult game at the end of a poor season. Shrewsbury went 2-0 up in the first-half. Their second goal seemed to happen in slow motion as Terry Angus lost possession just inside his own half and the striker ran through, rounded Barry Richardson and slotted home as Angus tried in vain to stop the ball crossing the line. A 2-0 deficit was surely never going to be overturned by this Cobblers side and we contemplated life in the Conference, or possible extinction. What we didn't expect was the fairy tale that unfolded before our eyes in the next forty-five minutes. Player-manager Phil Chard pulled a goal back before Shrewsbury hit the post. Had that gone in it would have all been over, but then a new hero was born. Pat Gavin hooked home the equaliser and minutes later charged down the goalkeeper's clearance from a defender's back pass to score the winner off his backside. As that ball crossed the line it was pandemonium on the terraces. I just could not believe what I was seeing. I had never seen the Cobblers come back from 2-0 down to lead 3-2 and I don't think I have seen it done since. This really was one heck of a roller coaster ride. This was the first time the Cobblers have brought me to tears. It was unreal. At the final whistle we clambered over the fences to run onto the pitch to celebrate. It was just so fantastically brilliant it's difficult to get those emotions across in writing. When I returned home my mum said I looked like I'd been through a massive ordeal! The Cobblers have been involved in many big games since this one but I still regard this one as the most important ever. One other thing that stood out that day was the group of Bury fans in the main stand who were cheering the Cobblers on because a Shrewsbury defeat would put them in the play-offs instead.

**Glorious days out**

Some of the other happy away days would include the opening day of the 1992/93 season at Gillingham. It was Phil Chard's first season as player-manager and a struggle was expected, so to come back with a 3-2 win with Chard himself scoring the winner in the final minute was glorious. The 1-0 win at Cardiff in a pressure-cooker atmosphere in the Division Three play-off semi-final was another great away day. Mark Cooper's sending off looked like we would be happy to hold out for a 0-0 draw, but Sean Parrish ran from inside his own half to lob the ball over the keeper to secure a fabulous 1-0 first leg win. My brother lost his glasses in the celebrations, but thankfully found them unbroken, which was just as well as he was driving home!

On the subject of play-offs, the second leg of the League Two semi-final at Mansfield was another pressure-cooker atmosphere. Losing the first leg 2-0 the Cobblers needed a big turnaround at Field Mill. 2,500 Cobblers fans helped create a great atmosphere and almost unbelievably we went in at half-time 2-0 up. A great strike from Marc Richards and Chris Hargreaves header levelling the tie. Within a minute of the re-start Martin Smith scored a third and we were in dreamland. Mansfield fans were is despair while we were in raptures. It doesn't get any better than this. Sadly, two shocking refereeing decisions from Phil Crossley cost us and Mansfield pulled one back to take the tie into penalties. It was the first time I had witnessed the Cobblers in a penalty shoot-out and I was more nervous than I have ever been watching the Cobblers. Sadly, Eric Sabin missed his kick and we were down and out and very distraught. It was certainly a case of if only.

**Promotion party**

Oxford away in 2006 was also a special day. The 3-1 win virtually secured promotion to League One under Colin Calderwood. I had purchased my inaugural season ticket the previous week – despite being a regular I had never had a season ticket, but with promotion imminent and tickets likely to be at a premium I shelled out the family savings. Because of this I felt the pressure of the promotion campaign. I really wanted to have bought a League One season ticket! Thankfully a magnificent all-round display against a struggling Oxford side, roared on by over 2,500 Cobblers fans, saw us run out 3-1 winners.

Promotion was secured the following weekend at home to Chester City that meant the final game at Grimsby was meaningless. Although not totally meaningless as Grimsby needed a win to secure promotion themselves and we wanted to spoil their party by having one of our own. There was a terrific atmosphere in the away end as again nearly 2,000 Cobblers fans sang and cheered throughout the game. For once there was no pressure on us. All the pressure was on Grimsby, big time. They got a fortunate penalty to go 1-0 up in the second half and that looked like that would be enough to win it and gain them promotion. However, they didn't reckon on what was to happen deep into stoppage time. With Grimsby fans set to party, some balloons were released as they thought the referee had blown for full-time. He had actually blown for a corner. From that corner, we scored the equaliser. How we laughed and cheered! The Grimsby fans were in total despair. That was probably the funniest thing I've ever witnessed at a Cobblers game.

I used to travel with the Cobblers Mounties or the St. James Travel Club, but the double-decker buses weren't the most comfortable! Nowadays it is the car (usually one of my brothers).

That completes some of my memories of following the Cobblers away from home. Following the Cobblers for over twenty years I have seen them play at the likes of Halifax, Scarborough, Barnet, Maidstone as well as the likes of QPR, Watford, Millwall and Forest. Wherever we go though I am always proud to be following the Cobblers.

**Lee Wade**

*Ryan Gilligan breaks Grimsby's hearts with a last minute equaliser at Blundell Park – (Pete Norton)*

## It Could Take All Day to Get There

I started supporting the Cobblers in December 1961, with my first match being a 5-0 win over Brentford and my first away match was a 2-0 win at Peterborough. The following season I attended most of the Saturday home matches with a group of lads from my home village of Wollaston. There would be about a dozen lads, ranging in ages of ten to fifteen and we would catch the Yorks service bus from Wollaston, get off at the Boys Grammar School in Billing Road and get to the County Ground at about 1.45pm. We could never go to night matches however, because there were no buses home after about 7.00pm.

After a year or so a space became available in a car, so from then on, I rarely missed a home match. Occasionally someone would run a bus to away matches, from the village, usually to "local derbies" at Peterborough or Coventry. I only missed one home match in the Cobblers 1st division season and went to away Leicester, Manchester United, Aston Villa and Spurs away.

**What the 'ell are we doing in Bridgwater?**
The following season I started going to away matches on a more regular basis, usually on United Counties coaches from Wellingborough. In those days there were no organised coaches to the long distance away matches, so when we played at Plymouth in September 1968, one of the regular fans organised a coach. We were leaving Northampton Market Square at midnight Friday, so we all met up about 8.00pm and had a few pints before getting on the coach. There was a group of fans who used to go to virtually all the matches and one lad called Willy had had too much to drink that night, so he was loaded onto the bus in a very drunken state when we left at midnight. We stopped at Bridgwater in Somerset at about four in the morning and Willy woke up and asked where we were. "Bridgwater" was the reply. "What the 'ell are we doing in Bridgwater?" enquired Willy. When we explained we were on our way to Plymouth, Willy replied, "But I'm not going today." He wasn't even booked on the coach but obviously there was no way back for him so we carried on. We arrived in Plymouth at 8.00am and got back at 2.00am the following morning. That same season we also went to Torquay for a Saturday night

game, leaving at 8.00am on the Saturday and getting back at 8.00am on Sunday. A twenty-four hours round trip to watch the Cobblers.

By season 1969/70 a friend called Alan Palmer from Irchester bought a car, passed his test and used to take a car load of us to most away matches. By this time I had left school and was working as an apprentice electrician. I was working in Cheshunt, Herts on the dates of our cup replays at Weymouth and Exeter. At this time I knew quite a few of the players (Phil Neal, John Buchanan, Ray Fairfax and Peter Hawkins). For the Weymouth replay, I got a train from Cheshunt into London and then down to Weymouth. The return train back was the *milk train* which didn't leave Weymouth until about 2.00am the following morning. After talking to Peter Hawkins about this he said "I'll see if I can get you a lift." This resulted with four of us coming home on the team coach, getting into Northampton about 4.00am in the morning.

For the Exeter replay, Alan was driving down so I got a train again hoping to meet him there, to get a lift home. I managed to meet him (no mobiles in those days) but unfortunately, he unlocked his car boot, left his car keys in his coat and put the coat in the boot, before shutting it. So we were stuck in Exeter at 10.00pm with the keys locked in the boot! We went to the local police station and they eventually came down with a big load of car keys and opened the boot. By now it was midnight and we faced a 200 mile drive home (pre motorway days). Alan was really tired by the time we got to Swindon and we told him to have a kip which resulted in three of us walking round an industrial estate for an hour, whilst he slept! We eventually got home at 6.30am, I got one hours sleep before going to work! That season is the only season where I attended every match.

**The Barton Cobblers**

In the later seventies I didn't get to so many away matches, because I was playing football on Saturdays, but I still got to most of the home games. I bought my first season ticket at the County Ground in about 1980 and have been a season ticket holder ever since. After moving to Earls Barton, I started to organise coaches to a few away matches each season. The first one was to Rochdale for the FA Cup 4th round match in 1990. Since that we have visited over forty different grounds with the Earls Barton Cobblers. The most nerve-racking trip was to Shrewsbury for the *great escape* match. We got to Shrewsbury quite early and some of us were in the bar of the hotel where the team had their pre-match lunch, although we had a different sort of lunch! On the way back we had booked into a pub near Gnosal, Shropshire, but we took a wrong turn and the coach finished going up a narrow lane with the hedge on each side brushing against the coach. When we got to the pub, we really celebrated with one lad, Martin James, sinking eight pints in the two hours we were there.

It can be hard work with the coach being full, you turn people away and then people drop out at the last minute. Another Earls Barton Cobblers trip that sticks in the memory is a trip to Boston United. We had only got as far as Thrapston when we received the news that the match was off due to a frozen pitch. We had a dilemma as we had booked into a pub near Spalding at lunchtime and we didn't want to let them down. After scanning the paper, we found that Northampton Spencer were playing at Deeping, so we decided to go to the pub and then onto Deeping. The pub was in the middle of nowhere and the landlord must have thought it was his birthday with over forty people knocking back the booze. Someone said "Will the match at Deeping still be on?" The landlord offered to ring and find out. "Match off" was the shout a few minutes later so we decided to stay in the pub a bit longer. We eventually left four and a half hours later and well-oiled at this point. When I looked at the paper the next day, the match at Deeping WAS played! Surely the landlord didn't tell us a porky to keep us there, did he?

We still run coaches to three or four away matches each season and these are always a good day out with a good set of lads and ladies.

**Roger Averill**

*The Barton Cobblers travel to Rushden in style!*

# One Day in Bristol

I was one of the thousand or so who travelled to The Memorial Ground for the first leg of the play-offs against Bristol Rovers, one of the thousand or so who suffered as The Gas went 3-0 up and one of thousand or so mightily relieved when a post stopped it being even worse. And then John Gayle grabbed us a lifeline with a well-taken lob over the keeper.

**3-1 and you...messed it up**

At full time, exceedingly grateful for this glimmer of hope, we started to file out and then the stadium announcer could not resist a chorus of "Wem-ber-ley, Wem-ber-ley." We all stopped in our tracks and looked up at the nearest loudspeaker, as if somehow, we would be able to identify the singer. He had insured a hostile environment would greet Rovers in the return leg and Ian Atkins' team talk was already half-formed. To this day, the song "Three-one and you messed (sic) it up" rings out during every Cobblers v Gas fixture.

Unbeknown to me at the time, one of the home spectators was my long-lost nephew Tim, an avid Gas fan and one among the many who, a few days later, traipsed dejectedly home from Sixfields after what I rate as the best Cobblers match I have ever seen.

**Nick, meet my Uncle Dave**

When Tim and I eventually re-established contact, football obviously became a huge topic of conversation and Tim has since accompanied me to several Cobblers home victories over The Gas, feeling the same level of fondness for Sixfields as does Ian Holloway. Of course, I have also been back to the Memorial Ground, to allow Tim some slight recompense.

On my first return visit to the Mem, Tim took me into the supporters' bar and introduced me to his mates, including Nick Day.

"Nick," he said, "this is my Uncle Dave. He's a Cobblers season-ticket holder."

"Bugger!"

"Dave has been here once before...."

"Bugger!"

"Dave, you'll hear Nick later. He's the stadium announcer. THE stadium announcer!"

"I'll have Northampton carved on my bloody tombstone," was Nick's response.

I thanked him on behalf of all Cobblers fans and he accepted this gesture as magnanimously as he was able. He also commented that his faux pas was mentioned very regularly by his so-called friends, who openly admitted that they were the sort of people who would keep bringing up the most embarrassing incident in Nick's public life.

I have met Nick on several occasions since and he's a very nice bloke. I don't really think that he should be remembered for one ill-judged moment in the euphoria of his club's seemingly safe passage to a play-off final. And then I think, "Yes, he bloody should." And what greater epitaph can anyone have than being part of Cobblers folklore?

Dave Blake

## My Son Almost Played For The Cobblers in Europe

It's not very often that you get to see your team play in Europe, especially when they've been confined to the bottom two divisions for the majority of their history, but in the summer of 2004 a few hundred Cobblers fans descended on the Spanish city of Seville for the club's pre-season tour. Ok, it wasn't quite the glory of the Champions League, but it offered a unique opportunity to get close to the action and meet the players.

The pinnacle of the trip was to be a third fixture at Seville's Olympic Stadium against a side called Vecindario. Only a year before, Celtic had been defeated by Porto in the UEFA Cup Final on this very pitch. Alas, there was to be a change of plan! The pitch at the Olympic Stadium was unfit to play on, so the game was switched to a training ground next to the stadium. The travelling contingent was gutted, but was offered a free tour of the stadium to try and make up for it.

After wandering around the stadium, we made our way to the training pitch only to learn of the second change of plan, which meant nothing to us at the time. Instead of playing Vecindario, Town would now face Spanish third division side Cerro Del Aguila. The first half was extremely one sided as the English side lead 5-0 at half time, some fans had stopped watching and started sunbathing in the 35+ degrees evening sun.

The second half was equal to the first half as Cerro Del Aguila barely touched the ball and became increasingly frustrated. Goal after goal followed and us fans were running out of fingers when the referee gave a penalty with the score at 13-0.

At this point my 13-year-old son Tom, who had acting as a ball boy on the running track, seized the opportunity for his moment of fame. After a quick chat with Colin Calderwood, the Cobblers boss agreed to bring Tom on to take the penalty.

*The newspaper clipping from the Chronicle & Echo the following day Town had their previous game in Seville abandoned when the referee walked off after an opposition player refused to leave the field after being sent off for a crude challenge on Tom Youngs.*

He was given the kit and lined up on the touch line to make his Cobblers debut. The crowd of a few hundred had now all sat up to take notice and a few were even chanting his name. Even the referee was ready to authorise the substitution, but there was still a spanner in the works, the Spaniards were having none of it. After a few minutes of trying to convince the captain that he would only come on and take the penalty then go straight back off again, they still wouldn't play ball. The excuse was *what if the keeper saved it and your son got* injured in the rebound? Tom was gutted and I was livid, but the Spanish third division side Cerro Del Aguila players were threatening to walk off the pitch at this point, so everyone backed off a little. Tom was then welcomed onto the bench by David Galbraith, who gave Tom his shirt. Steve Morison scored the penalty instead and Tom was content with shouting instructions from the dugout. The final score was 15-0 with the scorers: Tom Youngs (3), Steve Morison (2), Martin Reeves, David Hicks, Thomas Pinault, David Rowson, Ryan Amoo and Luke Graham. Tom Townsend's name could have appeared on that list too, if it wasn't for 11 sore losers. Despite not making his Cobblers debut, a hot Seville day proved a lifetime memory for a 13-year-old and his dad. We may not have been following a Premiership team in Europe, if we were, we would never have been allowed this close to the action.

**Told by Ian Townsend**

## Eight Hours of My Life... Wasted!

**York 2 Northampton 1**

A League Division Three match played on March 26th 1993. I'd never been to York, so I fancied this Friday night fixture, especially as work commitments also allowed me to go. A friend and I drove up to Northampton and caught the Mounties coach. We left at about 4.30pm and I remember thinking that it was a little late traffic wise for a Friday night, but we made good time and by about 7.00pm were on the outskirts of York. We passed one sign for York, and then another which said, CITY CENTRE, and I thought this driver obviously knows exactly where he's going. Oh yeah!

**Kidnapped by aliens**

Finally, we entered the city, still in plenty of time for the kick off. Another ten minutes went by and now we seemed to be in the city centre, and there in front of us were the old Roman walls. The coach couldn't continue, and in an effort to turn around, or take a detour, whichever, (at this point even the driver wasn't sure, so...) we had to take a right turn down a narrow side street. As we inched our way through the parked cars, we weren't sure if the driver was using his mirrors, or just checking that they were still there and that he hadn't ripped them off yet. We managed to negotiate our way back on to a wider road again. We were still lost, but now we were getting lost faster. Then someone at the front of the coach had a brilliant idea, no, he didn't invent the sat nav, unfortunately, something much simpler. Or should I say somebody though much simpler? Because walking down the street minding his own business was a lone York City supporter - at least, he had a York City scarf on - and we pulled over and beckoned him onto the bus. It's not quite up there with, *kidnapped by aliens*, but, in fact, might have been the more unusual, *kidnapped an alien*, as communications between driver and supporter suggested he might indeed be from another planet.

We went from the jubilation of thinking, now we'll surely find the ground, to the realisation that the guy we'd just picked up, was either,

a) Someone with no sense of direction.

b) Someone who'd just mugged a York City supporter for their scarf.

c) Someone who had just been beamed down from Planet Zog where they all wear scarves identical to York City supporters.

Frustration was now getting the better of people as kick off was by now fast approaching, and we were not. The supporter from Planet York didn't seem to know how to get to the ground, but to be fair, he probably didn't think he'd be directing a bloody great coach there. Either way, he was now getting plenty of abuse from the back of the bus, which started of good humouredly, but as time ticked on, got somewhat worse. There was a growing feeling we should stop and chuck him off again, or just chuck him off, stopped or not. The match had now kicked off, unless of course the York City ground had actually vanished, and that's why we couldn't find it. That bloody David Copperfield had a lot to answer for.

**Run, sprint, walk**

Suddenly the bus ground to a halt, and we were told something like, 'It's down there', or, 'This is as close as we can get'. Peering out into the darkness of York's backstreets, I could see no sign of a football ground, not even floodlights. Anyway, we left the coach, wondering if we would ever see it again, and set off by foot in the direction given. Some sprinted, some jogged, some sensible supporters accepted they had already missed some of the match and another five minutes wouldn't make that much difference, and walked.

My friend and I started off sprinting, unfortunately he was considerably younger, and considerably fitter than me, and I made the mistake of trying to keep up with him, thinking the ground could not be very far. I sprinted, I walked, I sprinted, I walked. My lungs hurt, a lot. I was convinced at one point we were just chasing the York supporter from the coach and there was no ground at all. I was now reduced to just walking, subject to abuse from my friend concerning the level of my fitness. Abuse I still suffer to this day whenever we relive these memories.

And then in the distance there it was, a ground, floodlights, the bloody lot, like an oasis in the desert. I managed a final sprint and arrived at the turnstile barely able to stand, and feeling that my lungs had been ripped out, and stamped on by a herd of African elephants. I just hoped that York Hospital was easier to find.

We paid and went in, the Cobblers had already scored, and we'd missed it. I could still barely speak and for the next fifteen minutes my breathing was such that I sounded like a pervert practicing his heavy breathing technique on the phone.

It wasn't a great game; York equalised and then took the lead. Something miraculous happened after the game. We were reunited with the coach. We were even allowed to sit on it and not run alongside it. We even had a collection for the driver - although what he really needed was a recollection, a recollection of where he was actually driving the coach to - but what sort of road atlas he could buy for 30p I don't know. Another eight hours of my life wasted, but hey, I'm a Cobblers supporter, I'm used to it by now.

**Nigel Wheatley**

*Happier times at York City's Bootham Crescent. Cobblers fans spill onto the pitch after a 0-0 draw on the final day of the 1997/98 season, a result secured a play-off place for the second season running. Around 3,500 Cobblers fans made the journey to witness a nervous 90 minutes of football, but this was probably one of the most celebrated goalless draws in the club's history.*

## Weird & (Not So) Wonderful Places

One of the great things about following a football team is the fact that you get to go to some weird and wonderful places that you wouldn't normally bother with. I'm not sure that I would have ever felt the need to go to places like Scunthorpe, Doncaster or Gillingham without the main purpose of watching the Cobblers, with my husband Mark. I would imagine that many football fans over the country have the same outlook on Northampton too.

There is one such journey that I felt the need to share with you just for the sheer strangeness of the whole episode, it normally raises a laugh whenever it is told to non-footballing friends.

On 11th April 2003, we sadly had to attend a funeral in Merseyside so made the journey up the M6 on the Friday morning to meet some family who were already staying up there. As the Cobblers were playing at Port Vale the following day, we decided last minute to stay over in Stoke on Trent that night to save going all the way home only to battle with the traffic on the Saturday.

**We emptied our valuables from the car**

After an emotionally moving service and wake, we headed for Stoke, arriving around 5pm with the next task in hand, to find somewhere to stay. Not knowing the area, we headed straight for the Tourist Information Centre in the City Centre. They were extremely helpful and booked us into a place called the Wheatsheaf Hotel in Hanley. Following excellent directions, we found this hotel nestled in amongst rows of semi derelict terraced houses just outside the city centre. Parking just far enough away from the gang of youths staring at us, we emptied the valuables from the car and made our way into the hotel. We were checked in by a friendly, if a little rough girl and shown to our room. She explained that the room was a little dated as they were refurbishing the hotel, but we didn't care too much as it was only a bed for the night.

After setting down our bags, we decided to venture downstairs to the bar for a pint, after all it had been quite a harrowing day on our emotions. Now I will build up a picture for you of this place. The bar was very spit and sawdust, with about twenty or so locals strewn around chatting after a hard day at work. Many were labourers who enjoyed the down to earthliness of this place as they supped back what was probably their fourth or fifth beer of the day.

As we ordered a beer each, two guys at the bar started chatting to us and enquiring where we were from and what we were doing in Stoke (or Hanley as they kept referring to it as). We told them we were going to see the Cobblers the next day and that was it, we were in a football conversation, as one of them loosely followed Vale.

After an hour or so a few more friendly locals had joined in our conversation, which now included pottery as one owned a ceramics business. One such local was very odd looking, he reminded me of Paul Merson's brother with a huge beer gut that looked like he hadn't washed for a good few weeks and had a rather large tide mark around his neck that probably came off the large fake gold chain he was wearing. He introduced himself as the owner of the hotel that we were staying in and welcomed us on board. He was amusing, full of half cut stories about people who had stayed here and telling some funny, but inappropriate things about his wife.

**He looked like Charles Hawtrey gone wrong**
As a few more pints slid down, we noticed a man walking, well actually hobbling towards the pub, assisted by crutches as he only had one leg. Now this guy looked like Charles Hawtrey gone wrong. You know, the funny fella from the Carry On films with the round glasses. Somebody joked that by the time he reached the pub, he'd be in time for last orders. Then the Vale fan piped up and informed us he was the bar manager, to which everyone fell about laughing. Two minutes later, the one-legged man was behind the bar organising things for the night, he actually *was* the bar manager.

If you have ever watched Fawlty Towers, you can probably understand what this place was like. All we needed now was Sybil to appear and low and behold, we didn't have to wait long. Within a few minutes a stern woman appeared behind the bar with rage in her eyes. She struck fear into the group that we were talking to, especially Paul Merson's brother. He described her as a **** sorry I cannot print the words. It was now complete! Basil was drinking with us; Manuel was setting up the bar and Sybil had arrived with fire in her belly and a deranged look in her eyes. She grabbed Basil across the bar, slapped him across the face and if I cut out the swearing, she told him to stop drinking and get on with preparing the food. He sidled back over to us, only turning around to tell Sybil how much he loved her too before finishing his pint. "I told you she was a ****", he said smiling.

We declined the offer of dining at the Wheatsheaf, despite the high recommendations of the locals and made out way into Stoke city centre (or Hanley) for a bit of Cantonese Cuisine. Our love affair with this wonderful establishment climaxed the following morning as were woken at 7.30am by the colourful cursing of three builders in the next room apparently refurbishing the place.

**A win would give us hope**

If we thought the weekend could not possibly get any stranger, we made our way to Vale Park that afternoon for a must win game for the Cobblers. Defeat would all but relegate us back to League Two, but a win would give us hope of staying up.

Trailing at half time, Marco Gabbiadini equalised for Town on the hour and the visitors went in search of a winner. Substitute Lawrie Dudfield smashed home what everyone thought was to be a last-minute winner and become the turning point of our season. Well almost... The home fans made their way to the exits, angrily chanting "Horton Out!" Within seconds of the restart, Peter Clarke headed home Vale's equaliser. By this point, about 30% of the home support was present to cheer the goal. If that wasn't a low enough blow, Adrian Littlejohn smashed a winner past Lee Harper pretty much straight from kick off again. From taking the lead in the last minute, the Cobblers had somehow lost the game.

As we walked through the streets of Burslem after the game, a bloke in a Vale shirt came up to us and said "Did we win 3-2?" Mark's reply was something along the lines of ok mate, don't take the mick, but he genuinely didn't believe the score line as he'd been one of the "Horton Out" brigade.

We never thought we would ever witness a game quite like this for some time! Cue Whaddon Road 5th September 2003, almost five months later and Town lost to two last minute goals at Cheltenham after going into stoppage time leading 3-2. It still didn't match the strange weekend in the Fawlty Towers near the Vale of Burslem. I am eternally grateful to my husband for taking me to some of these weird and wonderful places.

**Jules Kennedy**

## Oh I Do Like to Be Beside the Seaside

**Southend United v Northampton Town - April 12th 2008**

Last time I made the trip to Roots Hall to watch The Cobblers we lost 2–1, with Eric Sabin bagging a goal in the last ten minutes. That was the only highlight for what was really a 2–1 thrashing.

I have followed Northampton since I was a lad. Born in Northampton in 1980, I moved to Ipswich in 1982 but have always (because of my father) supported the Cobblers. I normally manage to get to ten home games a season and a couple of away adventures.

My next adventure to Southend, five of us set off from Ipswich station at 11.00am. Our party consisted of one true Cobbler, two adopted Cobblers, and two people who wanted to get drunk. With 24 Carlsbergs in tow which I believe we just about finished by the time we hit Southend, their mission was well and truly accomplished before it began. By the time we got to the stadium we were all pretty merry and I personally fancied us to nab a draw. The game was good, 1-0 up is always good away from home and although it ended a draw all in all very pleased with the result.

After the game we set off back to the away supporters' pub and stayed there until around sevenish before moving on to Southend town centre. By the time we were scheduled to catch the last train back we were all pretty drunk. We had a change over at Shenfield station and we had been recreating the wrestling days of The Ultimate Warrior and Hulk Hogan much to the disgust of the other passengers, you can't blame them really. As we bundled off the train at Shenfield, one of the adapted fans decided it would be funny to shut the train door with two of us still on the train, one of which as me. No problem I thought just press the open-door button and all will be well... It had locked and my mate and I must have looked a picture as we tried to prize open the door from the inside then the train started to move. I could see the other three rolling around on the floor with laughter while we had ultimate rage in the carriage. Well about an hour later as we pulled into Liverpool Street Station in London and the hangover starting to kick in, it said 12.30am on the clock and nil trains back to Ipswich. We managed to jump on a train to Colchester which stopped at Chelmsford for an hour before jumping in a taxi home which cost us £25 each. By the time I hit my bed it was 4am. To make matters worse, the following afternoon, I was in a corporate box for the Ipswich v Norwich local derby, entertaining customers who were not impressed when I was sick on me prawn cocktail starter.

Steve Ward

*Martin Smith misses a penalty in a 2-1 in October 2004.*

## Play Off Drama - Claret Version

One night stands alone in my memories as the night that summed up everything that it is to be a Northampton Town supporter. One night that captured the passion, heartache and pure emotion that following the Cobblers brings. That night was at Field Mill, 20th May 2004.

The Cobblers had sneaked into the play offs in the 2003/04 season as Colin Calderwood turned around a disastrous start for the club under Martin Wilkinson as we looked to bounce back from relegation from League One the season before. Calderwood took us into sixth place in the table with a final day win over Mansfield Town at Field Mill.

**We'll see you all next week**

Ironically, this meant that we would *see them all next week* and lined up against the Stags in the League Two play-off semi-finals. The first leg was a more than forgettable affair and after goals from Rhys Day and Junior Mendes we lost 2-0 at Sixfields, handing Mansfield a seemingly clear route to Cardiff's Millennium Stadium for the final.

What happened in the second leg is thing of Cobblers folklore and remains the most emotional game of football I have ever witnessed. All the talk before the game was that it wasn't over yet and of the incredible fight back against Bristol Rovers back in '98. But surely it couldn't happen again...could it?

I remember the deathly silence on the coach as we pulled up to Field Mill. Cobblers fans had sold all of their tickets, over 2,500 of them, to witness what would turn out to be an epic encounter. I looked at my dad next to me and I knew that he was thinking the same as me and that this wasn't just going to be a normal evening of football.

After thirty-six frustrating minutes and with the game still goalless, we grabbed one from nowhere. Marc Richards rifled in a shot with his right foot and we were right back in business! Being 1-0 up at half-time would have been a great score to take in but it was to get even better with three minutes left of the half. Chrissy Hargreaves connected with a low cross from the right-hand side and headed home to make it 2-0 on the night and 2-2 on aggregate.

**Nerve-jangling**

The claret faithful couldn't believe what was happening in front of them as the whistle went for the break and the atmosphere in the away end during half-time was extraordinary as disbelieving phone calls were made, nerves began to jangle and people started to believe that this could be a very special night indeed.

If we were dreaming at half-time, we had to really pinch ourselves a minute into the second half. Martin Smith picked the ball up on the edge of the area and curled a majestic shot into the corner of Kevin Pilkington's net. 3-0! And for the first time we were in front on aggregate.

For twenty-two minutes we were on top. It looked like destiny was calling us to Wales and a meeting with Huddersfield Town in the final. It seemed to just be going all too right for the Cobblers. And then came the controversy that started the heartbreak.

**Thank you, Mr Crossley,**

Tom Curtis fouled Eric Sabin on the half way line. Referee Phil Crossley seemed to give us a free kick but then he consulted both linesmen, then the fourth official before incredibly gave the decision the other way.

Curtis was on a booking and should have been sent off, something that would have surely seen us keep the advantage. But the free kick went the way of the home side and suddenly Mansfield were attacking. And who else but Curtis got on the end of a knock down and scored for Mansfield, levelling the tie once again with a quarter of the game to go!

With away goals not counting double, the tie ended 3-3 on aggregate and meant that extra time loomed. A clear penalty claim on Derek Asamoah's charge through on goal was waved away by Mr Crossley in stoppage time to further enrage the Cobblers fans and we had to settle for extra time.

Despite a nervy extra half an hour, the whole season would rest on a penalty shootout and I can honestly say it was the most nervous I've ever been whilst watching Northampton Town. After such an extraordinary game of football, for it to rest on this was heart wrenching. Martin Reeves, Martin Smith and Paul Reid all netted as the shootout reached 3-3. Then up stepped Eric Sabin, a man who had played a massive part in getting us to the playoffs. Sabin's shot was saved by Pilkington and we knew it was over. Even though there were still a couple of spot kicks left you could feel the deflation in the Cobblers end. Ironically it was Colin Larkin, later to be of the Cobblers, who struck the winning penalty and sent Mansfield through. As 2,500 travelling fans showed their appreciation for an incredible effort, some were reduced to tears. My own tears were of pride, tears that I couldn't hold in, when the chant of "we're proud of you" went up.

**Painful experiences**

People who don't follow football will always wonder how something like this can make you so emotional. But after 48 games, so many miles travelled and so much money spent in supporting your local team for it to end like that was one of the most painful experiences in my life so far.

It took a hell of a long time to get over and watching the DVD of the game now still gives me goose bumps. But the memories of eleven claret warriors fighting with everything they had, epitomised by the likes of Sammo and Hargreaves, coming so close only to lose it on penalties was Northampton Town summed up in 120+ minutes.

**Dan Brothers**

*Scenes from the final game of the season, The Cobblers beat Mansfield 2-1 at Field Mill to book a place in the play off semi-final, against the Stags. (Becky Brushwood)*

## Play Off Drama - Yellow Version

It was a night that none of the two sets of supporters would ever forget and even now when I see my mates in Northampton, we always have a little conversation about that dramatic night which unfolded at Field Mill

**The build up**

Most of us had days off work who were going to the big game as we started going around the town pubs about 1pm that Thursday afternoon with others meeting up with us about 5pm that evening. The atmosphere around Mansfield town centre was immense. The conversation in the pubs was "We've done it, we've done it we are going to Cardiff" as the Stags were firmly in the driving seat taking a 2-0 lead from the Sixfields leg. The clock was ticking down and the blood was boiling. The songs were pumping as fans started making their way up to Field Mill for what was the biggest game the town had seen for many years. Inside the ground it was chocker, even with twenty minutes until kick off the atmosphere was fantastic, both sets of supporters were in good voice which is something I do not experience very often at Field Mill.

**First half**
The first half started with Mansfield pushing forward looking like they wanted to finish the game early Wayne Corden actually scored but the goal was ruled out for offside, Junior Mendes adjudged to have been offside although he never even touched the ball. A five minute spell just before the interval saw the Cobblers level through Marc Richards and Chris Hargreaves. At that stage I thought that our hated Chairman, Haslam had paid the players off and I was in tears when the half time whistle went. The interval was quiet and in total disbelief underneath the stand it was hard to know what to say and all we could do is basically sulk in our pint pots for 15 minutes and listen to the Cobblers fans celebrate in the away stands.

**Second half**
The second half started as the first finished with the Cobblers on the attack and scoring more or less straight from the restart, which sent the travelling support whappy. It was unbelievable how a game could suddenly turn on its head. There was to be another twist, Tom Curtis should have been sent off for an earlier incident and ironically it was him who levelled the game and took it to extra time with a drive into the goal. As Curtis's shot hit the net, I went absolutely mental, suddenly the game was alive again for the Stags. Chances came and went for both sides, but the tie went into extra time.

**Extra Time**
Extra time was very even with not many chances just both sides having lots of possession but the main talking point was Alex Baptiste's tackle on Derek Asamoah. It looked a blatant penalty from where I was sat but everyone has their opinion and so did the ref Mr Crossley and still I think he bottled it because it was so late in the game. My heart was in my mouth as Asamoah hit the deck and I was mighty relieved when the ref waved play on. I still can't believe it wasn't given. The game ended and went to penalties all players shook each other's hands and every fan in the ground applauded the efforts of both teams.

**Penalties**
The Stags won the toss to have the penalties at the North Stand end of the ground, in front of the Stags fans. It was the Cobblers started the

shoot-out! It was heart-stopping tension for whole ground and millions listening to their radios and TVs. All ten penalties were on target, with the vital difference being Pilkington's fine save from Eric Sabin's kick and then Colin Larkin's which sparked wild celebrations at Field Mill

**Aftermath**

So the Stags were on their way to Cardiff. It was a night of unbelievable drama and tension. Both teams did superbly to recover from the dead and the standard of football was worthy of a higher division in a pulsating occasion. Over the two games, I thought the Stags just about deserved their victory but it could have easily gone the other way. At the end of the game, both sets of fans applauded each other, in recognition of the closeness of the game and the mutual respect for each other's efforts.

**The night out after**

The atmosphere in town was electric in most pubs they turned the music off so that the fans could sing and sing they did. It was a night that will live long in the memory of myself and other fans around the town, but it could so easily have ended with the Cobblers being victorious. Since that night I developed affection for Northampton Town and have been to watch the Cobblers on numerous occasions. That night at Field Mill saw a classic cup tie style game which football was the winner. The Cobblers fans were awesome that night and have been great to me ever since, making me an honorary Cobbler.

**A beautiful friendship**

Since the Play Off Semi Finals between my team Mansfield and Northampton I made quite a few friends, mainly through Cobblers message boards. One day, it was one of those spur of the moment things, I put my name down for an arranged day out to Darlington and had a great time. Since meeting up with these people they have been going on about the huge hate between the Cobblers and the P*sh, so I took it on myself to go to a local derby just to compare if it's in the same category as Mansfield and *Cheaterfield*. The Stags have always had a problem with the Spirites due to them being in Derbyshire and due to the miners, not to mention the time they broke our hearts in the play-off semi-finals in 95 with them then going on to win promotion, which I still have not really recovered from. But to this day I will never know how they hate Sheffield

United more than us they are way out their league while we are just two teams never to do anything and will probably end up like this for ever unless we get a Russian tycoon come in for us. Until speaking to some Cobblers I had never met, I never knew P*t*rborough used to be in Northamptonshire so now I know why the Cobblers hate *Boro* so much. Since my two early visits, I have found myself having regular days out to watch Northampton and really enjoy meeting up with a few friends at Sixfields or on the road. Many of them have been really supportive, especially after Mansfield's demise over the last few seasons, going through hell with a rogue chairman and then losing our football league status. I think that Cobblers fans can have a lot of empathy after what happened in the dismal days in the early nineties.

As the Stags have now parted company with the so-called chairman, I say here's to more friendship between the Stags and the Cobblers and good luck to all.

**Sean (The Stag) Revill**

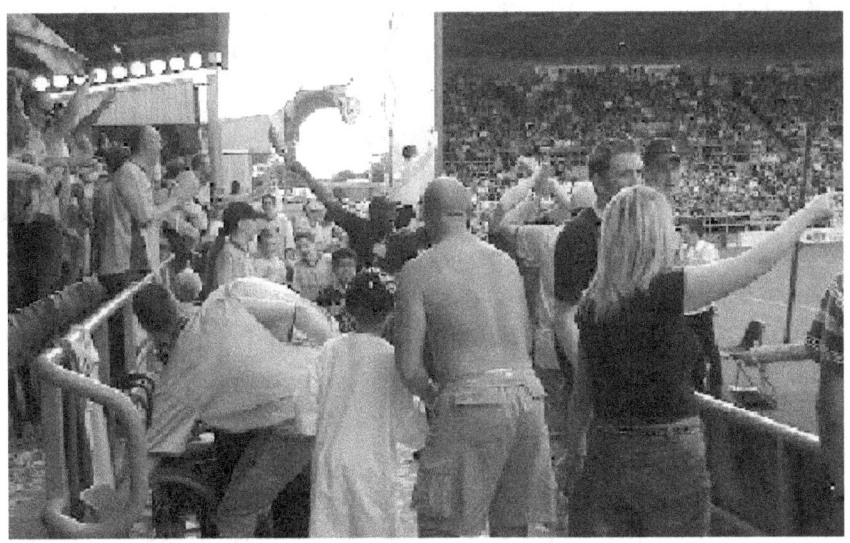

*Shirts off in the sun! Stags fans in the away end at Sixfields for the first leg of the play off semi-final (Ollerton Stags)*

# A Long Proud Trip Up North

**Newcastle 2 Northampton 1**

This was our third round FA Cup match in 1987, and came in the promotion season, when Graham Carr's Cobblers team flattened everything in its path. The tie was to be played in early January, but was postponed several times due to bad weather, although everyone suspected it was because Newcastle were trying to get star player Peter Beardsley fit, to play against us.

The previous two rounds had seen us dispose of unknown Anglian team P*terborough United 3-0, followed by Southend, a memorable, truly exciting, 4-4 draw at Roots Hall, and a 3-2 victory in the replay, courtesy of two (dubious) Gilbert penalties, McGoldrick and Morley winning them.

**After much pleading with a work mate, I got the afternoon off**

I had driven down to Southend after work, in torrential rain in a Mini Metro, so had initially decided I would hire something more substantial to drive to Newcastle on the Saturday, with two friends. However, several postponements later, the game was now scheduled for Wednesday, January 21st. By now, the car hire had been abandoned and as I left for work that morning I still didn't know how, or if, I would get to the game and if it was played, as the weather was still awful. Plus there was the added complication of it being my youngest daughter's seventh birthday that very day. During the morning at work someone who lived at Rushden reckoned there was a coach leaving a Rushden pub at 2.00pm and there were two seats left. After much pleading, I and a work mate somehow got the afternoon off and after getting back to Burton Latimer where I lived, my wife dropped us off at said pub where we duly claimed those two precious seats. It was still touch and go on the journey up there, the weather was bleak, there was still snow at the sides of the motorways, and fog would descend periodically. Even so, we made it to the outskirts of Newcastle by about six o'clock, joining a convoy of Cobblers coaches for our entry into the city under police escort.

To be honest I can't remember too much about the game. There seemed to be a hell of a lot of Cobblers supporters there, although we didn't make a great deal of noise as the away end at St James Park was still uncovered back then. The Gallowgate End, where the home faithful but they certainly made some noise, even though that was also minus a roof. Piles of snow surrounded the pitch, but surprisingly it played quite well, and the dreaded fog also stayed away.

The Cobblers put up a sterling performance, considering it was Fourth Division versus First, there was little to choose between the two sides. Richard Hill equalised, Trevor Morley was carried off and we conceded a soft winning goal, which was helped in by our new loanee full back John Millar. All in all, it was well worth the trip.

Back on the coach and a swift exit was required, but these were the days of rampant football hooliganism, and a big clampdown on alcohol on coaches had recently been introduced, with a zero-tolerance level. Suffice to say several police officers boarded the coach and conducted a thorough search, despite the fact there was no hint of any trouble. Worse was to come, they found some cans of lager in one lad's bag at the back of the coach. He was taken off the vehicle to be executed. Well, not quite, but it was some time before he returned, after presumably receiving a lecture on the perils of alcohol. Or at least, the perils of bringing it to Newcastle on a bus.

By now it was 10.30pm and we were still in the coach park in St James Park, so an early night was not in prospect. We eventually set off, and several of the more vociferous passengers decided we should now find a pub to get a drink. So we drove around Durham in search of one before they shut and a pub was duly found, only to be met with a rebuff, 'NO FOOTBALL SUPPORTERS'. So we headed home with our tails between our legs, and our tongues not far behind them.

I can't remember if we stopped at the services on the way home, but after persuading the coach driver to go out of his way and drop us off at Burton Latimer, I finally got to bed at 4.30am and had to be up again at 6.30am for work. It had been a long day - and night, and I had also completely missed my daughter's birthday, although I think she has since forgiven me. Luckily, she had her party on the following Saturday, so I had to miss the emphatic 5-0 thrashing of Rochdale at home, but it was a small price to pay.

**Like I had just emerged from a moshpit at a Sex Pistols gig**

Despite the atrocious weather conditions at both Southend, rain, and Newcastle, snow and ice, it was ironically the Peterborough tie at home, where I actually got the wettest. This was the game where the Cobblers decided to cram 6,000 home supporters into the Hotel End. Crowd marshals were in place to encourage us all to move towards the centre, and by three o'clock we were like the proverbial sardines. I had never before, or since, been so hot at a football match. I had to keep wiping the condensation off my glasses, and although it eased a little in the second half, I had to change my clothes when I got home, feeling like I had just emerged from the moshpit of a Sex Pistols gig. And the big away following supposedly coming from Peterborough failed to materialise, with the Spion Kop half empty.

Nigel Wheatley

*Newcastle's St James Park as it looked in the 1980's. The far touch line is dominated by the Jackie Milburn Stand, both ends behind each goal were open to the elements. The Toon Army pride themselves on being tough enough to brave all weathers though and could make some noise even on a cold wet Tuesday night. (Tranmere on Tour)*

# Loyalty and Despair

I have held a season ticket since 1997, although I have followed the club to every ground in the lower two divisions of the Football League since 1980 (well except Crewe). There are several words which could be used to best sum up what it means to be a Cobblers supporter (indeed most clubs except the glory boys who win everything at the top I guess). Words which spring to mind are: loyalty, despair, passion, frustration, pleasure, social, dedication, cost, togetherness. Some of these words sit well with some of the un-noticed things I have done in my past following this fantastic if sometimes frustrating club of ours.

**I'd be back in time for the Dukes of Hazzard or Knight Rider**
I take you back one such time and to the days of Graham Carr. The FA Cup third round and Newcastle United away. I was serving in the Royal Navy at the time aboard HMS Plymouth based up in Rosyth near Edinburgh. I had been fortunate enough to witness the fantastic second round games with Southend and the thirteen goals that those two thrilling matches produced. So, post Sarf-end, with kit bag in hand I headed back to the ship in Scotland and awaited the third round draw.

Total delight was the only way to describe my feelings when they drew out Keegan and Beardsley's merry men! A short one-hour train journey from the docks in Rosyth and I could meet the lads pre-match and be back on board in time for Dukes of Hazzard or Knight Rider! Brilliant!

Now bear in mind that this was pre-internet and pre-booking on the phone with a credit card...so there was a down side. I had to ensure I got a ticket, so the following week I took a day off work and jumped on the morning train from Edinburgh down to Northampton via Birmingham. I then got a cab to the County ground to buy my £3.00 ticket for the match. This had already cost me £50+ in train fares! Happy with my purchase, I then headed off back to Scotland...yes, I seriously did a day trip to get my ticket as it was one per supporter only!

So, you get the story. Newcastle then cancelled the match due to a frozen pitch...or was it they were running scared because Beardsley and a couple of their other superstars were not fit? It was re-arranged for the Tuesday night. Not a problem, or so I thought! As I awoke on the morning of the match, I was naturally filled with pre-match excitement. Four Geordie lads onboard also had tickets, so the five of us were looking forward to a few beers in Edinburgh Waverley before catching the train down to St James Park and possibly a few Newcastle Exhibitions in "The Strawberry Pub" before I met my mates coming up on the coaches.

**This is your captain speaking**

We awaited twelve noon with anticipation, jumped out of our working gear and slapped on the Sergio Tacchini track suit tops and trainers! The next minute was the most annoying in my entire seven years of serving my country. I quote from Captain Voute on Jan 21st 1987:

"Captain speaking. It has come to the attention of the FOSNI (Flag Officer for Scotland and Northern Ireland) that there is higher than normal Soviet activity in the North Sea towards Iceland. The activity has been seen as pushing the boundary of expected behaviour in clearly defined UK waters and as such action will be taken. FOSNI has directed that ourselves, HMS Rothesay, HMS Active and HMS Manchester will form a task group by 2359 this evening and head towards the Soviet fleet to discourage their presence in UK waters. The helicopter will be recovered from RNAS Culdrose within the next three hours and will carry out surveillance ops above the Soviet fleet in due course. Therefore, all leave is cancelled until further notice. Assume NBCD State 3 Condition Yankee, prepare for sailing at 1800 hours. That is all!"

WHAT??? How??? WHY??? I was gutted? Can you imagine? The hours on the train to get the ticket, the build up of excitement, the tension of going to St James Park to see the Cobblers only for me to now look forward to 30ft waves, rain, night time watch keeping looking at radar screens for hours and no Newcastle Exhibition beer either!!!

That night was terrible. We could just about pick up a medium wave transmission of Radio 2 Sports Extra but really had no idea what was going on! When the result did eventually get to us the Mags onboard were themselves saying "*What did you expect?*" and "*class tells.*" I will never know what that goal celebration was like when Richard Hill netted, still, that shows why I used the words at the top of my story describing what supporting the Cobblers means.

That one game amongst all the hundreds I've seen since 1980 summed it all up. I look back at that and realise how everything seems so much more exciting when you are younger (I was nineteen at the time). Whilst I don't feel old still, I guess at forty-one I am getting there really. So a word of advice for the younger supporters who moan about anything and everything on the various media these days. They will whinge about pie meat content, ticket giveaways, player signings, Northampton Saints Rugby fixture clashes, kit changes or even the club badge! Just enjoy the football, enjoy the social and sing loud for your team. Life is not to be taken so seriously guys. Your passion for the club is undisputed...but one day, there will be much bigger things to worry about in your lives and football will become a thing to wind you down...not wind you up! One day you'll look back on the late 2000's and think it was the best time of your life...even if you do miss a game through no fault of your own!!!

**Glen Cousner**

Glen's original ticket for Newcastle United v Northampton Town.
The FA Cup Third Round tie was eventually played on 21st January in front of a crowd of 23,177 with the Cobblers bravely bowing out 2-1.
Newcastle legend Jackie Milburn was quoted to have said,
"Northampton will obviously win the Fourth Division Title
and next year you can win the third as well."
Town beat Posh 3-0 and Southend 3-2 (after a 4-4 draw) on the way to the third round tie in 1986/87.

## Cobbler in Exile

The last two stories tell tales from the Cobblers' visit to St James Park (Newcastle not Exeter), this is a ground that became very familiar to me in the mid-nineties. Following the great escape at Shrewsbury, I moved to Tyneside in the summer of 1993. As mentioned, my girlfriend of the time lived up there and I was offered a job within Nationwide Estate Agents, as a trainee estate agent. It was extremely hard leaving my friends and family behind, but also my football team.

I managed a handful of Cobblers games that season, but working alternate Saturdays made it difficult to come home for weekends. My boss wasn't exactly flexible, in fact, if you asked to swap a Saturday, she would make sure it was impossible to do so. I started playing Sunday League football up there and was surrounded by a team of Toon Army fans who barracked me week in week out as I told them of another defeat. It must have been a depressing time to watch the Cobblers, but it was even less fun being a couple of hundred miles away and being the brunt of all jokes.

I tried talking all the lads into going to a game for a laugh. Well they could all laugh at me I suppose. The date was pencilled in, 26th March 1994 at Feethams. Darlo were a couple of points ahead of us, so I promised them a real basement clash. It was all too much for them as I found myself standing in the away end on my own. They all found excuses not to come along, but I am sure they were gutted to miss out.

As I arrived at Sunday League the next day, I got the usual question "How many did you get beat by then?" I was delighted to tell them that we won by virtue of Ray Warburton's twenty-first minute header. How we took the p*ss out of the Darlo fans next to us as we had finally climbed off the bottom of the table for the first time since about October. How we even got mentioned on 606 and their beloved Radio Newcastle. The latter reported on the round up, *"..and Darlington have gone bottom of the football league today after a 1-0 defeat to Northampton. Great news for Northampton fans, not that there will be any listening to us."* I would have called them if I knew the number and if there was a phone box handy. David Mellor then opened 606 by finishing his summary with, *"...and Northampton are finally off the bottom of the football league for gawd* knows how long. Are there any sad Cobblers that want to give us a ring tonight?" I wouldn't even dignify that one with a response.

My Newcastle mate, who indeed loved taking the micky out of my Northampton accent and insulting me by calling me *Cockney* or *Brummie*. Mind you, just accuse them of being a Mackem and that soon shuts them up. Anyway, they never did understand the day that we said goodbye to the County Ground.

**Goodbye County Ground**

Luckily the 30th April was a Saturday off from selling properties in Washington, Tyne & Wear, so I got Mum to sort me a ticket out for the last game at the County Ground against Chester City. It was an emotional day, coming back home, meeting a few mates on the Hotel End for the last time ever and taking in the last game to be played at our three-sided home. Funnily enough, I broke my pre-match routine and went for a beer in the County Tavern beforehand. I had arranged to meet my mum in there and collect my ticket, so I parked my car up did just that.

The Hotel End was absolutely buzzing that day, it was like a cup atmosphere and I had a tear in my eye as the teams came out for one last time. The start was perfect, Efon Elad played a ball down the wing to Kevin Wilkin, who smashed an unstoppable shot off the far post from 25 years. The whole place erupted with only nineteen seconds gone. That was that, it ended 1-0. The traditional end of season pitch invasion was extremely emotional as everyone seemed to wander about aimlessly and take in a whole lot of memories. Even the Chester fans joined us on the pitch.

We were back at the County Ground for four more games the following season, but the Chester game was officially my last there. There would be no goodbye part two for me, I would have to read about the Mansfield game on Teletext.

**Hello Sixfields**

If there is one way to annoy a Geordie, that is to jump the queue and get a ticket to a match at St James Park and leave him outside. Well I was missing football too much and got the chance of a season ticket to watch Newcastle in the 1994/95 season. I'd kissed goodbye to estate agency and moved into insurance sales which meant no more Saturdays. I was delighted and thought, why not, let's go and watch The Toon.

The season kicked off, but my first game was at Belle Vue to watch the Cobblers opener against Donny. We lost 1-0 and the usual ribbing came *"Going for another bottom of the league finish again"* or *"What a load of Cobblers."* I teased them with a riddle though. I told them that Newcastle and Northampton had something major in common that season but nobody could work it out. In the end I gave them the answer... Ballast Nedem! This construction company was currently working on the redevelopment of St James Park and were also building Sixfields. They weren't hugely impressed.

Anyway, I fought and fought for my ticket for the Sixfields opener on 15th October against Barnet. Mum had queued for tickets, but had to leave as the line didn't appear to move. I rang and rang and rang but all I got was the engaged tone. Finally I got through one Saturday at 9.50am, but was told that the computer was offline and would not be open until 10am. The lady explained that the problem with the phones was sorted and I would get straight through as there no queue outside. I rang back at 10.01am and got the engaged tone again. Now fed up but desperate to get to this game, I soiled my reputation and rang the opposition. The lady at Barnet FC informed me that they had plenty of tickets left and took my details. When I gave her my address, she said "Wow I didn't realise we had a Bees fan living that far away." The feeling of being unclean really hit home then, but it didn't matter, I had a ticket for the game.

**Bloody Barnet again**

The big day arrived and I made the trip to Northampton in my little red Vauxhall Nova. The excitement was immense as I pulled off the M1 and hit football traffic heading into Sixfields. No time to go home and see Mum first, I parked up in the North Car Park and headed straight for the ground. I got my first glimpse from the top of the hill and noticed it was pretty packed already. It was weird heading towards the away end, but I joined the queue in the South Stand with my lips tight. An announcement came over the tannoy that the game was delayed slightly due to crowd congestion. The Barnet fan in front turned around and said "What a sh*thole, fancy not being prepared for a sell out." It was as much as I could do to stay quiet and ask him about the state of Underhill. How dare he call Sixfields, this shiny new stadium, a sh*thole?

**Sit down, shut up**
I made my way to my seat, which was on the end of the row in the back row, right next to a steward. The two chaps next to me were moaning about the lack of leg room. Ignore them, I thought to myself. As the teams came out together, I applauded the Cobblers of course, but who would know next to me? The two chaps next to me then decided to strike up conversation which was all I needed. They started talking about Barnet players and performances in previous weeks and asking my opinion. I sort of avoided eye contact as much as I could, it was really hard to be unfriendly. Then the defining moment arrived, after sitting on my hands for the fourth or fifth time we hit the woodwork in the game, Martin Aldridge scored the first ever goal at Sixfields. It couldn't be a tap in or a bundled effort. No, it was a top-drawer lob and a somersault celebration to cap it off. A moment of real glory and it had to be celebrated. I leapt to my feet and was just shouting yeeeaaaarrgggghhh, when I managed to turn it into an aaaarrrghhsh*t and pretend to be gutted. A few of the North London contingent were up in arms about the fans that was on the pitch celebrating, so I thought it best not to bring too much attention to myself, but then I suddenly realised who was sitting to my left. That's right, the steward. He sort of sat me down discreetly and said "Ok mate, I know you're not Barnet, just keep it quiet though."
I smiled and he smiled back and winked. Dougie Freedman's equaliser was sickening, nine-hundred or so Barnet fans celebrated whilst I sat there in my seat. I think I was then well and truly rumbled, but the Bees fans were happy. They had grabbed an undeserved point.
The Sixfields experience was a great one and it made me want to go back for the next game, but funds were tight, so I had to make do with Premiership football week in week out. That season, I went to every Newcastle game. I knew one of the head stewards at St James Park and he offered me a season ticket at cost price. I had to pretend to be a massive Toon fan to get it, but I needed my football fix. Every week I would stand there in awe of Peter Beardsley, Rual Fox and co, but desperately trying not to think too much about the events at Sixfields or wherever the Cobblers were playing that day. No mobile phones meant that I would have to wait for Teletext at home to find out the Cobblers score. St James

Park would only give out the Premiership results as you were leaving the ground and there was no chance of making the classified check in the pub. A few beers in *Luckies* pub in the city centre would leave me hungry for the score. By the way, the name *Luckies* sounds worse that it was, it was a sports bar and not necessarily a place to get lucky in.

*They're actually building it, not knocking it down! Known as "The Meccano Stand", it was constructed in 1985 and surely the envy of every club around the country. This handy flat pack kit comes complete with instructions and a spanner for assembly. West Stand... no comparison! Sixfields couldn't come quick enough for this structure. (Pete Norton)*

# Chapter 5 - Why Do Fools Fall in Love?

If I had a pound for the number of times that someone asked me why I do it? Why don't I support a successful top flight team? Well I would be very rich now. In fact, I probably could buy a top flight team!

There is something of a love affair connected with supporting a team that is just around the corner from your house. Personally, I feel part of a community! I feel a sense of belonging! A sense of meaning! Sure, we can all look up the scores of a team that plays in a city that we have never been to in our life, we can all cheer loosely when that team wins on the television, but you can never say "I was there, I was part of that." I, like many of you reading this book, have many friends who decide on a route of glory, watching their team down the pub and celebrating winning another league title. They dream of lifting Europe's top prize again or witnessing the umpteenth league title in as many years, but to me, unless you are part of it, the whole experience is meaningless.

To win at Wembley in 1997, to survive at Shrewsbury in 1993, to beat First Division Coventry in 1990 and to beat administration, these are all things that I have been part of. To me, watching lower league football is more exciting. You must be mad; I hear you say. But how many different teams win the league? How many upsets are there each season? How many teams are promoted, relegated and then promoted again? It's an emotional rollercoaster for supporters at this level.

**Never a dull moment**

To summarise Northampton's plight since I have been attending. We won the league in 1987, almost made the play offs in 1988, escaped relegation in 1989, were relegated in 1990, threw away promotion in 1991, nearly went out of business in 1992, escaped relegation from the Football League in 1993, finished bottom of the Football League in 1994, started a new era in 1995, consolidated in 1996, won at Wembley in 1997, missed out at Wembley in 1998, were relegated in 1999, promoted in 2000, flirted with the play offs then relegation in 2001, escaped relegation despite being bottom at Christmas in 2002, relegated in 2003, made the play offs in 2004, and again in 2005, promoted in 2006, consolidated in 2007 and achieved above our level in 2008. There is never a dull moment being a Cobblers fan. There may be some depressing moments, but never a dull one!

I mentioned to you before that I tried the big club thing and supported Tottenham as a kid, but it meant nothing. I never saw them, so what was the point? I have taken friends to the County Ground and Sixfields over the years and, whether or not they return, they always understand the experience. They understand my passion for the club.

When I moved back to Northampton from Newcastle, I realised that a massive part of my life had returned when I walked through the turnstiles at Sixfields. Sure, the County Ground is now just a cricket ground. The buzz dozers had flattened our beloved mess of a ground, but the sense of belonging had returned. My first game back was a 4-2 League Cup defeat by West Brom in 1995, but I felt at home. After a year of watching Newcastle, I realised that the expectation level was different back home. We were never expected to beat the Baggies and we didn't, but everyone was proud of the performance. That was it; I couldn't wait to play Torquay in the next home game.

It was a little strange at first, having a pre-match pint at the Washington Square and even having to drive to games, but it was my team that I was watching week in week out now. Sure, it was great to see some real legends at St James Park, but it wasn't the same. The previous season I had seen Ian Rush, Alan Shearer, Ian Wright, Jurgen Klinsmann and Bruce Grobbelaar play against Newcastle and it was a real honour to see those players. I knew I would rather watch Jason White, Andy Woodman and co take on the might of Rochdale on a cold Tuesday night any day.

**It's good to be back**
The season began with goals! Yes, that's right, Ian Atkins and goals in the same sentence! The first two home league games saw a 4-1 crushing of Bury and a 3-3 draw with Mansfield, either side of a brave 4-2 defeat to West Brom in the League Cup. Watching football at Sixfields was a dream again. I was in my element, who needed Newcastle and Premiership football when we had a 'million pound' promising player on our doorstep in Christian Lee? We had a forward line that included Jason White, a bandy striker who ran wound like a headless chicken but managed to bang in a few goals. Chris Burns and Dean Peer had similar physique and Roy Hunter gave us that bite in midfield. At the back, Ian *Sammo* Sampson and Ray *Razor* Warburton dominated and of course Andy Woodman in goal gave us the spine of a great future. We were now reminiscent of a Graham Carr side, a team based on team spirit. Ian Atkins certainly knew how to get the best from his squad. I was lucky enough to meet the whole Wembley 1997 squad in the players' lounge after the 10 year reunion and every single one of them was still beaming when you talked about that day and their achievement on 24th May 1997.

**Unfashionable**
Ian Atkins was a great character and achieved so much as a manager. His unfashionable way of turning a struggling team into winners was certainly working its magic at Sixfields now and that suited me fine.
It wasn't all 3-3 draws and 4-1 wins though, as many Cobblers fans who watched this side know, there were a lot of 1-0 hang on for dear life as the claret back eleven scramble the ball away from the opposition's twenty-fourth corner of the game as our centre forwards makes his fifth goal line clearance of the half victories.
I remember one match against Plymouth when I dragged myself to Sixfields suffering from chicken-pox. It was extremely cold and I felt awful. We had one shot on goal to Plymouth's thirty odd and won 1-0. It was all

about picking up points and certainly not about finesse. It was frustrating at times, but most of the time it was funny. Everyone now hated playing Northampton Town because we were so bloody hard to beat. But it started to win the fans back...

In this chapter, we will meet some fans who tell us why they do it! They share with us what made them become hooked and why, after all those years, they still turn up for more punishment.

# A Fan for All Seasons

My earliest memories of the Cobblers and the County Ground are of Tommy Fowler in the late fifties, early sixties. My dad had taken me and from then on, the County Ground would play a large part in my life, both as a spiritual and an emotional epicentre.

As I began my footballing spectatorial career, Tommy Fowler was ending his playing career. A loyal servant to the Cobblers, he apparently used to greet visitors to the club, take their hats and coats and pour them a drink and he lives downstairs underneath the stand. He could still deliver the goods, an authentic left winger with an excellent cross. I watched the spectacle from the stand close to the Spion Kop end, absorbing the wonderful atmosphere. Here was all forms of human life; men, women, children, the young and old, the smart and the scruffy. To come from a small village as I did, where two people and a cat was regarded as a riotous assembly, and see so many people together for a common cause was incredible. Of course, it was also therapeutic, one could vent their frustrations on a player, the referee or the poor linesman, who was the closest target with no means of escape. There was no teacher here to tell you to be quiet and parents didn't expect you to be seen but not heard here. Here you were expected to be heard and you had no choice. You could be the lone star and shout out something which drew admiring glances and guffaws from others, or bask in the anonymity of the crowd and just join in hurling abuse at the dirty sod who'd just put Tommy into touch. That was what was so good about it, you didn't have to be clever and you didn't even have to make sense.

One shout I particularly remember from the lone star category was directed at Theo Foley. Theo was having a terrible time trying to mark his winger. This was unusual, as whatever his faults he had as a manager, the number of wingers that got past him in a season could be counted on one fingerless hand. In fact, people looked at one another in disbelief at such a sight. Except on this occasion, when the rather less than helpful advice from the terrace was *"Sh\*t on his shoelaces Foley."* Needless to say, Theo couldn't comply with these wishes, the winger wouldn't stand still for long enough to start with.

All this reverie and camaraderie combined with the wonderful aroma of pipe tobacco smoke drifting over proceedings (this from a non-smoker) created an atmosphere of sheer joy, filling the senses. Tommy Fowler mesmerising another fullback was simply the proverbial icing on the cake. As I said, I lived in a small village, Great Addington, which is some twenty miles away from Northampton, not a great distance granted, but sometimes difficult to complete. We never had a lot of money so we didn't have a car, although my dad had a motorbike. However, this wasn't always practical as my mother was never keen on riding pillion, particularly in poor weather. We tried various alternatives, by United Counties bus, but it was a laborious journey involving a change of vehicle and a tour of Northamptonshire's lesser beauty spots.

A far more enjoyable mode of transport was by steam train. This was before Beeching's mutilation of British Rail when he closed many outlying stations in rural areas. The nearest station to us was one at Ringstead, stuck in the middle of nowhere. So for a Saturday game, we would probably set out at about nine o'clock for the three-mile walk through the meadows and across the River Nene (we would even use the bridge sometimes). A strange sight for cattle en route. (Oh come on, you must have seen a bemused cow)? Although when I started taking a ball for the cows to play with, they were soon up to the level of the cows on the Anchor Butter advert on television. Some thirty years ahead of their time. So avoiding numerous cowpats - you would think if they can be trained to kick footballs, they could also be toilet trained. Perhaps I should have collected some for Theo Foley in case he had another tricky winger to mark later on in the day. Thistles and inquisitive animals cleared; we'd wait for the lumbering giant to chug into the station. As the distant train got louder, the billowing smoke grew thicker, our anticipation and excitement grew with it. On the journey the ticket inspector would always say something stupifyingly obvious like "Are you going to the football then"? There I was bedecked in enough claret and white wool to render half a dozen sheep naked and he had to ask. I always wanted to reply, *"Well no, I am a child model attending a knitting convention in Northampton"*, but of course I didn't, I was far too polite.

On arriving at Northampton, we'd have a walk around the shops, religiously have our dinner in Littlewoods before catching a bus to the ground. One thing that's always intrigued me about the County Ground, and I must confess to my shame, I do not know its history, is why it is that ridiculous size. Much too large for either a cricket or a football pitch, but not quite big enough for both. My dad also used to take me to County Cricket matches. This was in the Milburn, Lightfoot, Crump era. Fine crickets all, but the Northants players were always a bunch of players of physical extremities. Brian Crump, I've always loved that name, was very short, especially compared to Brian Larter who was 6'7." Albert Lightfoot had a hooter that was so large that he was the only cricketer to be given n.b.w. - nose before wicket. Once the umpires stopped play for bad light until they realised that Albert was fielding directly in line with the sun. And Colin Milburn was the Billy Bunter of English cricket, but what a marvellous player, and the minutes silence before a Cobblers match a couple of years ago, was one of the most finely observed I have ever witnessed.

I was a keen autograph hunter and built up a good collection. Most cricketers were very obliging; the best time to secure signatures was at lunch as both teams made their way to the pavilion across the football pitch on a diagonal route to the County Tavern where lunch awaited. As I said, most were very obliging, but not all. At one match, nearly all the Worcestershre players had put open to paper but then I approached Tom Graveney with my humble plea. *"Can I have your autograph please?"* Tom, big on talent, short on manners, snapped *"No, you're not allowed on this pitch, now get off!"* We were nowhere near the boundary, probably on the edge of the football pitch, about where Mickey Bell would weave his magic. So there I was, red carded off the sacred ground by an English Test Cricketer. So Tom, you stuck up miserable b*stard, may you lose your middle stump and never regain it.

There was an added bonus to watching the cricket, because by July the Cobblers players had reported back for training and were often at the ground. I first stumbled across a group of them in what used to be the old tea room at the back of the Hotel End. The resulting autographs of Terry Branston, Barry Lines, Mike Everitt and Frank Large brought me so much pleasure, but also some concern. Because the signatures seemed to suggest a fraud had been perpetrated on an earlier occasion. This was when a work colleague of my father, who I had never met, insisted that he had easy access to the Cobblers dressing room on match days. At which point he either offered or my father suggested that he could obtain the players' autographs for me. My autograph book was duly handed over and I waited for its return with eager anticipation. After a somewhat mysterious delay (with hindsight) of two weeks, my dad brought the book back from work. There to my delight were the signatures of most of the Cobblers first team. I cherished these signatures and showed them off with pride, and thought no more of it. That was until the fateful day in the tea room at the back of the Hotel End when I watched my heroes sign in person. Later comparing them with their original signatures, it became glaringly obvious that they were totally different, all of them. Also, on closer impaction, you didn't even need to be an expert on graphology to observe that the originals all more bore a remarkable resemblance, the loops and the crossed t's etc. So Terry Branston, Barry Lines et al were all one and the same person, my dad's work colleague. It was more disappointing in more ways than one, not just because I had been duped, but that a Cobblers supporter had lacked the imagination to write some with his right hand and some with his left, asked his wife to do a few and even hold the pen between his toes and scribble. Still I suppose that he wanted to keep his shameful deed a secret.

A few years later and due to my dad's ill health and the fact that I now have a car, it was my turn to repay him and take him to our beloved County Ground. We sat in the stand again after a lengthy spell on the Spion Kop. Although the Cobblers were in decline, there were still some enjoyable matches. This was in the time of Sunday afternoon matches in the early seventies.

Dad passed away in 1975 and went to the great football terrace in the sky, all though I suppose it's all seater up there as well now. I am sure he is still watching every game the Cobblers play, I dread to think. Something along the lines of "If this is heaven, what must hell be like?" Constant re-runs of P*terborough matches probably.

**Nigel Wheatley**

# You Can Take the Man Out of Northampton but...

There's a lot of pride in supporting your local club and particularly when that club's struggling away in the basement league, hidden away from the glitz and glamour that the Premier League provides. But when the local team is no longer local the sense of pride increases and this is a typical view shared by many Cobblers fans that move away for whatever reason. Back in 2003 my reason was that of university calling and I headed to Southampton with my Matalan crockery set under my arm and heavy heart for the town that I left behind. None of my new flat mates in halls of residence had any idea where Northampton was, let alone that it had a football team!

I realised how much pride it gave me after just a couple of days in that I was a Northampton Town fan as I mingled with new course mates over a drink in the student union bar. The usual suspects of Arsenal, United and Chelsea fans met me, littered with the odd supporter of Liverpool, Spurs and Villa.

**Comparing Europe to Oldham**

As they recalled classic European nights, I was comparing it to a cold Tuesday night at Oldham or the time that it hailed on us in the open terrace at Brentford just before Christmas. My stories were a million miles away from the ones being thrown in my direction but that was just it, they were unique and full of character. Plus, I was actually there rather than watching on Sky. I found myself trying to persuade some of my new friends to join me at a League Two game some time but in the end only two or three would ever take me up on it.

Anyway, the story of my university life would provide a memorable journey and an extraordinary pattern emerged as we rose from the depths of League Two. The first game on my arrival was very handily down the road as we had been drawn against Portsmouth in the League Cup. I missed the chance of a pub crawl to be at Fratton Park and as my flatmates recalled a drunken night on the town where they got lost and stole a bike, I looked back on a 5-2 defeat and a rain drenched away end! This is how it would go for my university years as sacrifices had to be made to accommodate The Cobblers' promotion hopes. But when I began uni life we were nowhere near the play offs even. The Saturday after Pompey and we were local to my new home again, this time at Oxford, and the writing was on the wall for Martin Wilkinson in a 3-0 defeat.

Wilko was gone soon afterwards and Colin Calderwood steadied the ship eventually. 2004 began with heavy hopes of a late play off surge and the excitement of the FA Cup run also put us in the public eye for once. The weekend when we played Manchester United on Sky made me very proud, despite the 3-0 home defeat, and won me a lot of congratulatory comments on return to uni.

The agonising play off semi-final defeat to Mansfield brought the curtain down on that season but I began year two at Southampton Solent with hopes of promotion this time around. Of course, it wasn't to be again and we crashed out in the semis once more, this time at Southend.

**A majestic day...**

And so to my final year and as I embarked on a massive few months academically, the Cobblers were looking good for automatic promotion this time around. Incredibly, we so nearly sealed it back at Oxford, the place where the story began just under three years previously as we won 3-1 at the Kassam in a majestic day all round that saw sun, passion and an away end crammed to capacity.

A week later and a win at home to Chester would give us a route into League One. Scotty's McGleish's header gave us the points we needed and the celebrations began. I rushed back to Southampton to celebrate in style with my housemate, a converted Cobbler from a Chelsea upbringing. That day back in May 2006 made it all worthwhile and if anyone ever asks why I don't just jump ship and follow Southampton I point to days like that. Nothing could give me more pride in my football team than donning the claret in a pub in Southampton, having people stare closely to work out who on earth I follow.

Home games have become as long a journey as some away outings as I travel on a five-hour round trip to get to most games at Sixfields. In the 2007/08 season I was at Leeds having been on a five-hour trip just to get to Elland Road and it was a six-hour journey back home in the end!

I know of more than a few Cobblers fans who continue to follow us from uni or from work in other towns and some call us mad for continuing to subject ourselves to travel hundreds of miles to witness debacles and defeats on the road. But it's all about pride and being behind your side wherever you are in the world, spreading the word like a proud father talking about their son. As someone great once said, *"You can take the man out of Northampton..."*

*Someone great may not have said this. In fact, it's more than likely they didn't, but it sounded good!

**Dan Brothers**

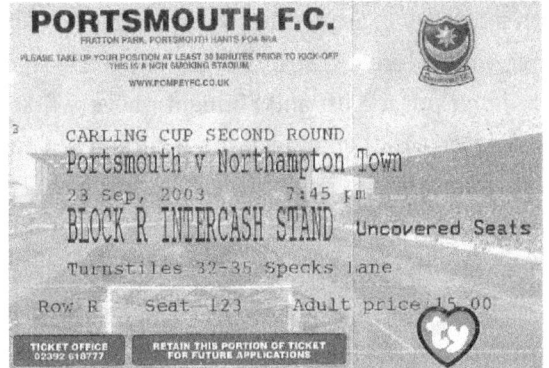

*Dan's first Cobblers game after moving to University*

## Not the Greatest Start

My first ever Cobblers game was actually a pre-season friendly, at Sixfields versus Chelsea on a Friday night in July of 1997. I had moved to the Northampton in April of the same year. Unfortunately, the reason we went to the game...my mum is a Chelsea fan. We lost 2-0, expectedly, but not as bad as a 7-1 thumping I heard about from the same team a few years prior to this.

My second game was not until 1999. I remember the date was 6th February. We played Blackpool at home and it ended 0-0. Three years later I randomly went to two games at Sixfields, Brentford and Cheltenham in late September/early October time. I think we lost them both 2-1 so it could be said that my first handful of games were not the greatest by any means.

I started to attend Sixfields more regularly in about 2003. One result that does stick out in my mind was a 5-1 thumping at home to Hull City on 4th of October, my 15th birthday. Not a very nice present. A Monday night Sky game at home to Swansea sticks out, I was one of the first there on a freezing November night and we beat the Welshmen 2-1.

**My real love affair started with a 2-0 defeat at Shrewsbury**

My real love affair didn't start until August 20th 2004; my first away game. I went on the coach to Shrewsbury and we lost 2-0. A week later, a trip to Scunthorpe which we lost by the same score line and then Mansfield. 4-1 to the Stags on a Sunday in September at Field Mill. My first three away games following Town were disastrous to the say the least.

Despite this, it didn't put me off and I bought my very first season ticket for the 2005/6 season. And what a season it turned out to be. One that brought me so many happy memories. Taylor's goal late on versus Torquay to send us into the top three, the win at London Road courtesy of Scott McGleish and the three amazing weeks at the end of the season. Oxford away when we won 3-1 and knew we'd be up with a win at home to Chester, we did win that game and the celebrations on the pitch afterwards. Then the nothing game in Cleethorpes where the whistle for a corner resulted in black and white balloons being prematurely and meaninglessly released. What a way to top off a promotion campaign.

There was little to write home about in 2006/7, a poor start to home form meant even a revival after Christmas would mean nothing, however, this was the season in which two events occurred that made me feel like a real supporter. August 29th saw us play Bristol City on Sky and to coincide with this game, a collection to raise money for the Trust. I was there in my t-shirt with a bucket and helping, in a small way, to keep the faith. It was around the time of the real hate against Northampton Borough Council for their delays to the stadium redevelopment and the fans needed to stick together. There were only a few there but those who turned up really made a difference.

The second thing was the protest prior to the visit of Scunthorpe on Easter Monday. It was so well publicised and a lot of people turned out for the march, I felt so proud standing outside the guildhall in my shirt and walking from town to the stadium (via Sixfields Tavern, of course) with so many other strong-minded people. Beating champions elect Scunthorpe in injury time remains one of the best days of my life for everything that happened on the day and in the game itself.

Moving to London in September of 2007 has stopped me seeing as many games as I would like, only three for the whole of this season. That doesn't matter though, my heart is still with the club and I know that one day I'll be a regular again. To the end of the 2007/08 season I have been to see the Cobblers play away from home a total of 38 times since August 2004. This figure will rise in coming seasons as I still intend to complete 'The 92'. My all-time favourite player has to be Scott McGleish. Despite some criticism, he could get a goal from nothing and managed to win headers against players twice his size. The guy never stopped running and had a great goal:game ratio.

In the future I hope we can get to the Championship and stay there at least. Anything is possible. I hope the hotel is built and ultimately, the ground improved. Fingers crossed.

**Sean Wilkinson**

## Most Enjoyable Thing I Will Ever Do

Having a father that has followed the Cobblers for 40 years, it was rather inevitable that I would end up supporting them as well. With me only being sixteen years old, you won't find much reminiscing of the good old days, as such, my earliest memory of the Cobblers is going to the opening ceremony of Sixfields, where I remember us releasing the Claret and White balloons. My first Cobblers game was more glamorous though. The Division Three Play-Off final between Northampton and Swansea is where I finally caught the Cobblers 'bug'. My first ever football match was at Wembley! Brilliant! Unfortunately, I can't remember any of the match, or John Frain's majestic free-kick which got us promoted. Luckily I've watched the video countless times. After that I attended a handful of matches over two or three years, including the Grimsby Play Off Final the following year. I was also lucky enough to go to Torquay away where we got promoted in the sunshine. I got my first season ticket for the 2000/01 season. That season I was mascot for the game against Reading, which we won 2-0 with a brace from my favourite player at the time Jamie Forrester. We played on the pitch for ages, got autographs and John Hodge even had a kick-about with us.

My favourite memory of the Cobblers has to be Rotherham away in the third round of the FA Cup. I remember the excitement of drawing Manchester United at home. Having grown up to know just about everything about the Cobblers, even at that age I knew that we always have a tendency to throw opportunities away. How wrong I was that night, as we not just beat Rotherham on their own turf, but totally outplayed them. As Rotherham scored, the old thought "here we go again" came into my mind, but Richard Walker and Martin Smith (*Son of Pelé*) scored and made all my dreams come true. We were going to play Manchester United!

At the other side of the scale, I wouldn't call it my worst memory, but it was certainly the most heart breaking. I'm referring to THAT night at Field Mill, where we were robbed by THAT ref. Despite losing, I was very proud of my team that night. We showed true spirit to go from losing 2-0 to be winning 3-2 on aggregate, before we were failed by an incompetent ref. The atmosphere from the Cobblers fans that night was awesome, and I wish we could replicate our away atmosphere at home more often.

I have only two regrets following the Cobblers. The first is that I didn't go to the County Ground and experience how bad it really was. I'm gutted that I never got to watch a match on the Hotel End and feel envious of those people that did and say how much better the atmosphere was. My second is that I didn't go to the Bristol Rovers Play-Off match at home, which many say was the best atmosphere ever at Sixfields.

There aren't many Cobblers fans at my school, so they cannot understand the considerable stress being a lower league fan puts you through. They are sitting on their comfortable sofa watching *their* Manchester United or Chelsea sew up another title. But they will never get the pleasure that I get from watching the Cobblers. I'm proud that I support my local club and have grown up with them. I may never see my team win the FA Cup or the Champions League, but at least I was at my team's matches! The glory hunters never had and never will have the experiences I've had.

simple ones like being sent a letter from the Ali Gibb Soccer School to say that once again I had got the question right, but hadn't been chosen for the course. Neither did they have the experience where I went up to get Sammo's autograph for about the 100th time (my dad was his kit sponsor) and he said, "Not you again...." That made my day. Ian Sampson, Cobblers legend, knew who I was!!! That's what is great about supporting a club like the Cobblers, you actually become a part of it and it is the most enjoyable thing that I will ever do.

**James Averill**

# A Computer Game Changed My Life

Imagine that you are playing a football computer game at home and this ends up being the thing that changes your life forever. Well that is exactly what happened to me! One day, I was playing the computer game The Sensible World of Soccer and a team called Northampton Town caught my attention. Not only by the claret shirt, that they shared with my home town team Benfica, but the Cobblers picked up some great wins that were so easy to get with that team. And what was curiosity soon became a habit, all football computer games that I played, I picked Northampton Town to be my team to undertake the ultimate challenge. Pretty soon, I tried to get more information on the Cobblers and the easiest one was, without any doubt, the highlights of Division Two on Sky News (the only Sky channel free in Portugal). Very soon afterwards, there was a boom in internet service in Portugal and this would be the last step required for the growth of a true and long-lasting love.

**Skipping lessons to watch Chris Carruthers play for England**

Around December of 2001, the NTFC website started to have one foreign visit on a daily basis. And, as an inquisitive mind usually does, I tried to get more and more information by the day. The message boards were the promised land as I was looking for. I registered on there and read it thoroughly, occasionally posting online messages. Still, I was surprised to have made an impression, when, after a few weeks people remembered me and my location! By this time, the Cobblers where my second love, and even though they came second, I would spend more time reading about it than about my first love Benfica. I would make some small sacrifices like skipping an all afternoon of classes in the university to see Chris Carruthers play for England in the Toullon Tournament.

All the glory and excitement of English football got the better of me, not the top end of English football, but the lower leagues, where English players are the majority. The amount of goals scored is more than in Portuguese football, the leagues have more teams, the games are more frequent, and the number of yellow and red cards is less. This love and wonder was so big, that one day, when Northampton Town played Norwich City, I found myself shivering in front of the computer waiting for the Sky Sports Score Centre would show the right goals. On another day, after the Rotherham v Northampton Town FA Cup replay, I found myself jumping in my bedroom like a madman, celebrating the words said on Sky News that night: "Full time at Millmoor, Northampton Town are going to play Manchester United." As I called my best friend for her to record on VHS the goals and Colin Calderwood's reaction, I heard this words that I'll never forget: "Calm down Luis, you are euphoric! Calm down!"

Of course, the dream to go to Northampton and see the Cobblers and meet all the friends I had spoken to over the internet soon became too big to not be done. So, for over a year, I started saving up money to do this. Of course, all realistic dreams have a price and one of them was the sacrifice of my season ticket of Portuguese champions Benfica, my number one team. Several details needed fixing and it was a hard task. English accommodation, transportation and beer are expensive from a Portuguese point of view, so the hard task of saving as much as I could was made better only by the thought of being at Sixfields and seeing the players in claret play in real life. All my friends from The Hotel End and Sixfields Boys message boards were more than kind in answering questions and giving advice. At the end, Graham from Sixfields Boys, fixed me up a caravan, a lift from and to the airport, and so much more. Then I discovered that another guy Steve arranged me a tour to Sixfields and a meeting with some of the staff or as I like to call it: HEAVEN!

**Sixfields was more beautiful than I'd ever imagined**

I arrived in England on the 11th August, Graham picked me up at the airport and we went straight to Sixfields, where while I was waiting for the tour, I met for the first time a couple of people I had been talking to online. After a pint or two in the Sixfields Tavern, I went to the tour of Sixfields. I saw Sixfields stadium for the first time ever, and it was even more beautiful than I ever imagined! There is something magical about the view from the hill, looking over the Dave Bowen Stand that still brings a smile to my face in any situation! While waiting it the Cobblers shop, I saw former players David Rowson and Andy Kirk. It was like seeing your all-time heroes, so I had my picture taken with the with the League Two's top scorer. Whilst I was still over the moon with that, the club press officer Gareth Willsher came to us to take us on the tour! Before I knew it, I was stepping the grass of Sixfields. The stands, the grass, the goals, everything was just perfect! After the tour I met Director of Football John Deehan, who was so welcoming and he quickly renamed me as Luis-Eusebio-Figo-Rui Costa! Standing next to John Deehan was Cobblers legend Ian Sampson and there was nothing more in the world besides this! I was meeting Ian Sampson and John Deehan! A few other players came over and posed for photos, taken by club photographer Pete Norton

John Deehan then gave me the opportunity of being tutored by him on the art of penalty, but I have to say I only scored one out of three. At this time any penalty advice would go in one ear and out of the other because I was too thrilled to think. It just couldn't get any better; I was the happiest man on the world when I finally met manager Colin Calderwood. As he got to me, he shook my hand and said: "Hello, very nice to meet you." I was completely thrilled but totally speechless. After two or three seconds, in which I said in a funny, trembling and over-excited voice: "Very nice to meet you too." I couldn't believe it I was shaking the hand of the Manager of the team in my dreams! It came as no surprise that I lost the penalty shootout with Colin Calderwood!!

**A regular face at Sixfields**

Sadly, my short trip to England ended too quickly. I took in two games, a goal less draw at home to Wrexham and a 1-1 draw away at Shrewsbury and but I was to return at the end of the season. In the time between my visits, I couldn't stop thinking about how great the locals were and how much the club accommodated me. You certainly don't get the same level of interaction with Portuguese football clubs. I returned the following April to witness the Cobblers beat Chester 1-0 and clinch promotion to League One. Another dream trip to Northampton, but the third visit was to be the most significant. After some bad times in Portugal, I made the decision to make the move to Northampton and found a job in a scientific company within my first month. By the time this has been written, I spent one full year in Northampton. I can assure you that time does fly when you are having fun.

Many people think I am mad, leaving a hot country, moving to Northampton, leaving family and friends behind but I know I have made the right choice. I had the biggest honour of all when I was voted "Supporter of the Year" at the end of the 2007/08 season. So the next time you play a football game on a computer, remember it could change your life!

**Luis Pereira**

# Thrilling in the Rain

My First Cobblers League Match - The day of truly fell in love with Football and The Cobblers!

**Northampton Vs Doncaster - Saturday 24th February 1996**

If ever there was a match to get me hooked on football and the Cobblers, this was it! I'd been to Sixfields before for a couple of mediocre games - one a friendly loss against Aston Villa, and the other an FA Cup win against Hayes, but nothing prepared me for the rollercoaster ride I was about to experience on this day!

**Peeing it down**

One Saturday with nothing to do, my friend and I decided a trip to the football was in order. With the clouds darkening and letting lose a barrage of rain, we made our way to Sixfields. We arrived and purchased our tickets, before racing through the turnstiles to take cover from the continuing rainfall. As the water fell from the heavens, we feared our afternoon's entertainment would not go ahead. A pitch inspection was then held by the referee who deemed that the match would be delayed, to at least see if the rain would ease up and the conditions improved. The rain eventually calmed and a delayed kick off time of 15:25 was announced. The delay to the game added to the anticipation, what sort of game would we get, particularly on a rather soggy pitch?

The clock then ticked 15:25, the whistle blew and the match commenced! Northampton raced into a two-goal lead inside the first fifteen minutes with goals from Ian Sampson and loanee Neil Docherty. The Cobblers looked set for an easy win, or so we thought! Then as the game approached half-time, Doncaster were awarded a penalty. Colin Cramb stepped up to take the spot kick, but a brilliant save from Andy Woodman denied him! But no sooner though had we caught our breath from that save, than another penalty was awarded for Doncaster, John Schofield took responsibility this time and scored. The whistle blew for the break, 2-1 at half time, the Cobblers still in the lead, just!

The second half began, Doncaster got another almost straight away through Colin Cramb. 2-2! All the hard work of the first half had been undone. Then mid-way through the second period, despite a strong suspicion of handball, Colin Cramb cracked in a second on the volley. 3-2 now to Doncaster! My friend and I could not believe the Cobblers 2-0 lead had now been eclipsed by Doncaster's three goals! What had happened? Surely though the Cobblers had one last throw of the dice in a game like this, and they did! As the match entered injury time, the Cobblers were awarded a penalty for a handball, Jason White stepped up to take it, some people could not bear to watch but the ball hit the back of the net for 3-3. The referee closed proceedings seconds later, the final whistle blew on an incredible game of football. 3-3! What an afternoon's entertainment! Six goals including two penalties scored, one saved, plenty of incidents and just think the bad conditions and a risk that the game would be called off. Who could ask for anything more? This was the day I jumped on the Cobblers train, and it will be a long long time before I get off!

Chris Evans - The Happy Cobbler

---

## Thanks to My Brother

I never really got this football game thing. Kicking a ball around, shouting, cheering and swearing, then getting in a bad mood when your team loses. For many years I had to put up with my dad and brother going on about Northampton Town, the team where they both originated from. Having grown up in Poole, Dorset, the closest team to me would be Bournemouth but for some reason Dad "hated" them. I used to get the promise of a trip to Dean Court when Bro used to come down to visit but always declined.

**I was talked in to it**

After leaving home, I moved to London and started working in a construction office where I was surrounded by even more mad football fans and after some gentle persuasion, I agree to go down the pub and watch England in the World Cup. Ok, I have to admit, it wasn't that bad, I actually quite enjoyed it. Bro was well impressed with this and tried to talk me into going along to watch Northampton the next time they played in London and I agreed to give it a try. For months on end I would receive texts updating me on the Cobblers progress and I started to take an interest in the club's progress. Dad started to become impressed too.

So I was all set to go to see Northampton play at Leyton Orient in January 2006. I had to ring my Bro and asked him what he was on about when he was talking about fans teams and fanzines and he said he'd explain this on the day. The big day actually arrived a week early as the Cobblers were drawn away at Crystal Palace in the FA Cup 3rd round. This was quite cool as I worked with a Crystal Palace fan. I made my way to central London to meet Mark, Jules and a group of their mates who were travelling for a big day out. I was introduced to a group of lads on the train and told that they were a fans team before being handed a magazine which was a fanzine. This was all starting to make sense now.

The short train trip to Selhurst was good fun and I quickly joined in the banter of the group. We then headed to a pub full of Cobblers fans quite close to the football ground. I was amazed at the camaraderie and spirit between everyone. Everyone seemed to know everyone and had such knowledge of what happened last week, last month or even in 1960 whatever. After a few pints (well I had wine, which I'm told is not normally a pre-match drink), we made our way to the ground. Inside I couldn't believe how many people had travelled from Northampton, there were thousands. The atmosphere was great, singing songs and chanting names. I was taught a few dittys and joined in the best I could. One of the lads lent me a claret and white scarf to wear too.

**The wise cracks and quick remarks**

As the game began, I was in stitches listening to the wise cracks and quick remarks from the people around me. Crystal Palace scored early on but this didn't dampen anyone's spirits. Moments later I experienced a huge rush as Northampton equalised through Josh Low (I wouldn't have remembered that if I hadn't asked). Everybody went crazy and somebody picked me up whilst jumping around to celebrate. I was complete bedlam, but it was amazing. Now I started to understand this rush.

Northampton ended up losing 4-1 but from what I saw, it was harsh, two penalties helped Palace on their way. The next thing that struck me was the spirit after the game, despite the defeat, nobody seemed in a bad mood. Everyone left the ground smiling and pleased with the way the team had performed.

A week later, I found myself getting up early to make my way to Leyton to watch the Cobblers fans team beat Orient fans 8-1 with my bro scoring twice. He told me this was a rare feat because he didn't score many, but it was nice to see the fans team in action after meeting them the week before. I then enjoyed Northampton's 2-1 win over Leyton Orient in the afternoon. Since this day, I have since been to Sixfields to watch a couple of games and find myself going through the pre-match ritual that many of you regulars experience every week. It is nice to meet up with people and keep in touch with some of these friends through Facebook to get regular updates on the Cobblers. I get regular texts from Mark and Jules when they are at games, so it is nice to feel part of the football culture now.

**Told by Katy Kennedy**

## Three Generations

The Cobblers run in my family as me, my dad and grandpa are all supporters of Northampton Town FC. We decided to put together some of our favourite memories from three generations. First, when did we start being Cobblers supporters? Grandpa started supporting the Cobblers when he was twelve, in 1934, my dad was eight, in 1972 and I think I started supporting the Cobblers when I was also eight in 2004.

**The first time**
Funnily enough, none of us can remember our first games. I can't remember the opposition in my first game against, or the score, but I can remember one thing, I asked Dad when David Beckham was coming on! Becks didn't make an appearance that day! All my dad remembers of his first Cobblers experience was being sent to stand at the front of the Spion Kop whilst his dad, my grandpa stood a few rows back and swore a lot. As for my grandpa, he can't remember anything about his first game at all, he says it was too long ago.

**The heroes**
We have lots of favourite players, I built a shortlist of mine. Josh Low I thought was a good player, he played on the right wing and I think was the best right winger I've ever seen in the lower leagues. In 102 appearances he scored 12 goals. Shame that Josh now plays for our rivals

P*eterborough. Martin Smith; he had a great left foot and was really good at free-kicks and Scott McGleish; He could score from anywhere at any time with 42 goals in 111 appearances for the Cobblers. I was also a big fan of Poul Hubertz, who just kept on scoring in the second-half of the season in 2007-08. Mark Bunn is a legend, who makes amazing saves all the time and is probably the best goalkeeper in League One.

**Star-struck**

Dad's favourite players were Paul Stratford who was a really good all-round player, Martin Smith who he thinks amazing vision and Steve Massey who he said behaved like an old-fashioned striker. Dad was also quite star-struck every time he met Martin Smith.

**A dream team**

Grandpa's famous players are Tommy Wells nick-named 'Shadow' because he was so fast. He played on the left wing from 1935-1939, Daniel Tolland; mostly known as 'Danny' Tolland, centre-midfield from 1935-1939, Len Riches right-back from 1935-1939, Jimmy Maguire, played right-back from 1935-1939 and Percy Mackie who came from Arsenal and was an Irish international. He also mentioned goal keeper Len Hammond, striker Albert Dawes, left back Fred Dawes, striker Ted Bowen, goal keeper Bill Gormlie; He played as goal-keeper, winger Colin Lyman and Welsh international John Parris. Most of these players played in the thirties when my Grandpa has his first season ticket. Does anyone remember these names?

**A classic match**

Looking back over the years, we talked about our favourite matches. My Grandpa enjoyed the Division One clash with Manchester United in 1965, which ended in a 1-1 draw. My dad's favourite match was when we beat Bristol Rovers in the play-off semi-final and he ran on the pitch afterwards. My favourite match was when we beat Swansea 4-2 and in the first 30 minutes, we were 3-0 up and Swansea were top of the league.

**Was he good enough?**

In 1939 my Grandpa actually had a trial for the Cobblers when the club put an advert in the Chronicle and Echo. They wanted footballers who hadn't been called up to fight in the war, to turn up at the County Ground at 7.30pm. About forty lads turned up but there was only one ball. He said he that he got a kick about every thirty minutes! The Manager, Tom Smith was sat in the stand and when Grandpa asked when they were going to split into teams but someone shouted "Tea Up!" and everyone went to the tunnel for a cup of tea and that was the end of the trial.

**Orin Willis (aged 11)**

*An original season ticket from 1938/39 season which was sent in by Orin's grandpa, Noel. The book consists of three sheets giving the first team fixtures and the second team, or reserve fixtures.*

This season, the Cobblers played in Division Three South and kicked off with three straight wins. A 2-1 victory at Torquay was followed by home successes over Watford (2-0) and Leyton Orient (3-0), who was then known as Clapton Orient.

The biggest win of the season came at the County Ground on 4th February in the shape of a 5-0 hammering of Aldershot, but exactly a month later, Brighton left the same venue with a 4-1 win.

Match of the season could arguably have been the visit of Mansfield in November who edged out Town to win 4-3.

# Memories That Mean a Lot

**My dad's fault**

I support Northampton Town thanks to my dad's influence. It was he who first took me to the County Ground and we stood on the Cricket Side, before that I had supported Manchester United but I saw sense in the end. Since then I have visited 94 league grounds and around 127 in total culminating in nearly 1,000 matches. In that time, I have had a range of Cobblers heroes, Steve Massey, Wakeley Gage, Trevor Morley, Ian Benjamin, Phil Chard, Neil Grayson and Scott McGleish to name a few.

Most fans who follow their team will understand when I say, going away from home to watch your side is always more of a day out then just turning up for home matches. The games never seem as memorable when you look back, although some particular home games will always stand out! Following the town for over thirty years there's so many good and bad memories, but here just a selection that mean something to me.

**Memories that left a mark on Northampton**

3rd May 1980 Portsmouth (H) lost 0-2 (Cobblers score first). My first real memory of the Cobblers, nearly 11,000 for the last home match of the season but there must have been over 8,000 up from Pompey to see them clinch promotion, they were everywhere except the Hotel End from my memory and they also left their mark on Northampton.

**Look away now**

22nd November 1980 P*terborogh (H) 1-4 – The FA Cup was really special in these days and you always got a bigger crowd. Started well took the lead through Steve Phillips, scored a great second goal by Peter Denyer (header going up with the keeper) but the referee disallowed it, Boro' never looked back and won the game 4-1. Let's say the locals weren't happy and it was my first taste of seeing the bovver boys in their jeans and boots ready for a rumble in Abington Avenue.

19th September 1982 Bristol City (H) 7-1 – missed the Sunday match as I had knocked myself out jumping a fence, one of the Cobblers biggest post-war wins and I missed it. I saw the 3-0 defeat to Bury the following Tuesday however.

**That's better**

12th October 1985 P*terborough (A) 5-0 – Travelled over to Boro' with the Mounties Travel in two green double-decker buses. The Cobblers were starting to play some great football (ahead of the championship season) and we over powered the Posh easily whilst being helped by them having their keeper Turner sent off for kicking Trevor Morley in the head! Did I enjoy this match and what a first every away match?

30th November 1985 Cambridge (A) 5-2 – Another derby game and another five goals with Benji getting a hat trick. I was getting hooked on these away games with performances like these.

11th January 1986 Mansfield (A) 0-1 – The game was at risk right up to the Friday due to snow. We lost due to a dodgy penalty in a bad-tempered game, which saw Richard Hill sent off. The police spoke me to in a tactful way, after gesturing to the Mansfield fans. They had more serious trouble later, after provoking a group of skins that followed the Town at the time and it took five or six officers to arrest one fan who wouldn't go quietly.

Unfortunately, that wasn't the end of the drama and we were kept in the ground after the match for approximately fifteen minutes, which didn't go down well. One elderly Cobblers fan had gone in their main stand, he'd gone the wrong way out when leaving and had hurried back thinking he'd miss the bus home, when he had a heart attack and sadly died. Not the best of matches to remember and the treatment received from the old bill and stewards, was just how football fans were going to be treated for the next ten years and we just took it as being the norm.

16th November 1986 P*terborough (H) 3-0 – FA Cup First Round and a big gate of over 9,000 saw the Cobblers easily beat the P*sh. I also think it saw Derek Banks arrive in a helicopter landing on the cricket pitch, which made a change from their cars on our side for once.

2nd December 1986 Exeter 4-0 (H) – I think was a Tuesday night match, in which we were the first team to hit the 50-goal barrier.

10th December 1986 Southend 3-2 (H) FA Cup Second Round Replay – End to end game with some great Morley dives to win us two penalties; bring on the Newcastle in round three.

28th December 1986 Cardiff 4-1 (H) – Christmas games always brought out the crowds but I don't think anyone appreciated the numbers that would turn up. Officially just over 11,000, but I have heard that there were over 14,000 in the ground, which was more than the capacity. The away end wasn't even full either. At times in the hotel end you were just lifted off your feet and you just went with the sway of the crowd.

26th April 1987 Lincoln (A) 1-3 – Some Cobblers fans were so drunk they were playing rugby with an empty whisky bottle before the game! Phil Chard cracked a stunning 30 yard goal but into his own net and we lost to the bottom side in front of around 2,500 Cobblers fans.

29th April 1987 Crewe (H) 2-1 – The long-awaited confirmation that we were champions. Pitch invasion at the end and celebrations by the players taking most of their kit off (not a pretty site in some cases). After the previous bad years of applying for re-election to the league, this was something new for me, promotion and silverware.

10th May 1987 Wrexham (A) 3-1 – Over 1,500 Cobbler's fans celebrating in Wales, we even outnumbered the home fans. Stopped off in Coventry on the way home and celebrated with plenty of beers and food. The Coventry fans only had one thing on their minds, the FA Cup final with Spurs the following week.

15th August 1987 Chester (A) 5-0 – In my memory we won the opening game 1-0 but most Cobbler's fans will say no 5-0. We were last leaving the pub in our convoy of buses and we broke down just outside the town (way before mobiles were around). A bus finally came to pick us up gone 4pm and I've never seen a bus fill up from front to back as quickly as this did. We got to the ground at 4.30pm and I then had an argument with the police, as they weren't initially going to let us in. They did finally and we saw the last goal of the 5-0 victory.

2nd May 1988 Sunderland (A) 1-3 – Great season for the Cobblers but we still needed more points to clinch a play-off place. Eric Gates stubbed his toe in the ground and won a penalty! But 30,000 fans applauded Tony Adcock's chip, the best goal of game. It was sadly not enough and Bristol City, Walsall and Brighton were all above us and in the play offs.

15th April 1989 Sheffield United (H) 1-2 – I will remember this match not for the best of reasons but due to Hillsborough happening that afternoon.

With mobiles not being around there was just rumours at half-time from people listening to their radios, even the announcement at the end of the game didn't really tell you of the severity of the event.

6th January 1990 Coventry (H) 1-0 FA Cup Third Round – Cup giant killers! It wasn't often that we played top sides, yet beating them too! Very wet and muddy but nobody cared after Steve Berry slotted in the first half winner. Don't mention round four and Rochdale however, there were rumours that some of the players didn't prepare properly and were playing cards late the night before - who knows?

25th August 1990 Hereford (A) 2-1 – A superb Kevin Wilkin volley and a Bobby Barnes goal gave me the bragging rights over new friends from Hereford. Where I was staying for the weekend and I celebrated with many bottles of Holsten Pils on the Saturday night.

18th April 1991 Carlisle (A) 1-2 – You don't always realise the importance when meeting new people following the Cobblers, met a guy today known as Gregg and thought this was his Christian name (until I was told it was Andy a year later) as that was what everyone called him but it turned out to be his surname! Great bloke and we have been good friends ever since, even to the extent that he was best man at my wedding 14 years later!

4th April 1992 Barnet (A) 0-3 – In the build up to this match with all the sackings etc, I wasn't sure if we would have a team to even play the match, so the result was immaterial. We sang our hearts out all the same and some of the players even threw their shirts into the crowd at the end, like we had won a trophy.

6th September 1992 Hereford (H) 1-1 – Opening home game on a Sunday, we couldn't beat a team that ended the match with only seven players! Did I get some stick after the game from my Hereford mates?

8th May 1993 Shrewsbury (A) – I don't think I need to state the score to any Cobblers fan. Except at half time we looked doomed, as the Cobblers don't do comebacks, we were just relying on my Hereford friends to do us a favour. But the second half is now history and their score didn't matter in the end, just Pat Gavin's a**e. It was Phil Chard's tactical switch and team spirit along with 2,000 roaring Cobblers fans (and a few Bury) helped. Big celebrations on the pitch and long into the night, in Milton Keynes of all places.

**Look away again**

16th October 1993 Scunthorpe (A) 0-7 – Steve Sherwood in goal say no more! To make matters worse one of my mates Andy Oxford paid £42 for a taxi to get to Northampton, as his car had broken down that morning. Sometimes it makes you wonder if the players truly understand what lengths fans will go to watch their team.

30th August 1994 Torquay (A) 1-2 – Lost again down in Devon on a Tuesday night, but the ten of us had a great night out on the town. To cut a long story short, two of us end up crashing into a pensioner's wall on the way home by the person giving us a lift as he was over the limit, he got arrested and we went to hospital with one of the girls that we had pulled (it was the front-page headline in the local paper the next day). Whilst Navy John ended up getting engaged within four weeks to the girl that he pulled that night, he broke it off as quick after she chased him with a carving knife after a slight disagreement one night (they are a bit weird in Totnes).

15th October 1994 Barnet (H) 1-1 – I never thought I'd see the Cobblers in a new home after all the years of talk since the sixties (I'm told). Great to see the ground so full but I still miss the Hotel End and the noise it could make. Just a pity we couldn't get a win what a goal by Martin Aldridge.

12th November 1994 P'boro (A) 0-4 – It was my mate's birthday up north but you couldn't miss an important match like this, so I compromised & went up for the Friday night but driving back down early Saturday morning. Let's just say the weekend wasn't the best, with my mate nicked for criminal damage and inside the nick on his birthday! Two others had to break into his house, as they didn't have any keys, so one climbed up the drainpipe and then lifted his girlfriend up & grazed all her stomach (as he thought the alarm was on but he could have just let her in the front door!). We got the keys from the police station and got home late and not in a great state. I then got up at 8am (probably not the cleverest idea ever) and drove the 150 miles back home to catch the bus to Boro'. Played reasonably well without scoring until they took control in the second half and stunned us with four goals.

13th April 1996 Preston (A) 3-0 – Anybody who was here that day will remember Larry's (Neil Grayson) hat-trick against the PNE, they were the league leaders at the time but we totally dominated and deservedly won.

11th May 1997 Cardiff (A) 1-0 – First ever play-off game and 1,800 Cobblers wet on the open terrace saw a class finish from Sean Parrish give us an important 1-0 lead, with only ten men as well. It was a typical Atkins performance, on the road, holding onto for a 1-0 victory.

14th May 1997 Cardiff (H) 3-2 – Great night, performance and atmosphere, result never in doubt. I still couldn't believe it in the morning that the Cobblers were going to Wembley.

24th May 1997 Swansea 1-0 – The whole day and atmosphere were obviously better than the match, which was quite tense and tight as no team wanted to lose with some much at stake. All it took was John Frain's free kick and history was made. We partied in London for a while before heading back to town and joining in the celebrations around town until the small hours of Sunday morning.

18th April 1998 Plymouth (A) 3-1 – We hadn't got a great record at Plymouth but a superb Chris Freestone hat-trick saw the Cobblers deservedly win with the last goal being made by Dean Peer running nearly the length of the pitch to set it up! The locals weren't happy and coins were exchanged between both sets of fans with their aptly named "top guard" stewards being in the middle of it.

10th May 1998 Bristol Rovers (A) 1-3 - Not the best performance and we could have conceded more than three with the game being over by the first leg, but a late John Gayle goal change all of that along with their stadium announcer! I think he was saying get your Wembley t-shirts organised now (or something like that). This didn't go down well with us fans and it obviously did Ian Atkins team talk for him too.

13th May 1998 Bristol Rovers (H) 3-0 – I've never known a night at Sixfields like this one. The atmosphere was incredible all-round the three sides and, in the pub, beforehand, everyone believed we would win. What was defender Ian Clarkson doing in the box to score one of the goals? More celebrations at the end and Wembley here we come again.

11th September 2001 Middlesbrough (A) 1-3 – Last away trip with the Cobblers Mounties (Les and John) before they packed up and what a day. The tragedy in New York took many people's attention away from the match, with the pictures coming through at service stations and on TVs at the ground. We played reasonably well but couldn't match Boro for their quality. It certainly was a very strange day.

10th April 2004 Hull (A) 3-2 – This was a new ground for me and an exciting match, with lots of great football played by both sides but the Cobblers caught them out with some early first half goals and held on to win. This was the first game that my girlfriend (now wife) attended with me and the start of an incredible run that saw the Cobblers win nine, draw two and lose only one match when she was there. The defeat came in the home leg of the play-off match against Mansfield when she bought her own ticket, so you can guess who bought the tickets after that!

**The good ol' days**

You may wonder why there aren't many recent games covered in my memories it's just that the early games mean more to me. Also, the *Mounties* who we travelled with disbanded after the Middlesbrough match, so the fifty plus regulars have had to find different ways of getting to games now. We now don't get lost finding the ground, breaking down on the coach, or just getting a thirty minutes beer stop, but that was just part of the experience travelling with the regulars who followed the Cobblers on the *Mounties* (you know who you are).

**Bobby the Cobbler**

*The sun shines on Cobblers fans on the English Riviera, but the away end at Torquay is sheltered by a huge flag.*

## Complete Madness

Some people like football and some people are total football nuts. But then, some people go beyond being football nuts, in this case Andy Gregg does just that. He has a passion for Northampton Town and you can guarantee that if the first team are playing, Andy will be there. By the end of the 2007/08 season Andy had clocked up 956 consecutive first team fixtures. The first game in this sequence was Hereford away at the start of the 1990/91 season. Andy tells his story;

"Funnily enough, my first ever game was at home to Hereford on 25 October 1986. I don't know exactly how many games I have been to, but it must be somewhere around 1,100."

Andy, who hasn't missed a home game since October 1987 due to a holiday, which he was not happy about, didn't really have any plans to set a record.

The last game I missed was Rotherham away at the end of the 1989/90 season. We had been to Tranmere on the Tuesday night and been relegated. I used to go to games with a mate who decided he wasn't going to go to Rotherham, so as I had only just started going to a few away games, and not knowing many other fans, I decided to give it a miss."

So how do you keep motivated to keep supporting a club in an era when it wasn't exactly filled with glory. Over a long year period, there must be times when you feel like giving it a miss. Andy has had that feeling on a number of occasions.

One game that always sticks in my mind is when we had just been knocked out of the FA Cup by Crawley on the Saturday and we were playing Reading away on the Tuesday night in the Leyland DAF/Mickey Mouse Cup. This was in the days when they were still playing at Elm Park. I used to travel with the *Mounties*, and we regularly used to take a full coach or two, but we only managed to fill a minibus for this game! It turned out we went on to win 2-0 and was a cracking performance, especially against higher opposition. There have been many other Tuesday night games (Plymouth, Torquay, etc in cup games) and you do wonder what the hell you are doing traveling all that way to watch a game of football!"

When football is in your blood, it is hard to miss a game. One year, Andy was on a camping holiday with a couple of mates. The Cobblers were playing Gillingham away in the first game of the season so they had to get up early on the Saturday morning and travel from Devon to Gillingham. Not an easy journey in anyone's book, let alone in a 15-year-old battered Astra! They only just made kick off and Gillingham scored in the opening minute Town did go on to win 3-2, so it made it all worthwhile.

A lot of people think that you're mad supporting a team like Northampton, but how mad do they think you are when you never miss a game no matter what?

**Swore at the teacher**

When I first started going, I was still at school and so I used to take a lot of stick off of mates, as in the early nineties, supporting the Cobblers was pretty depressing. One game that particularly stands out was a Tuesday night away game to Burnley. We got hammered 5-0, and as you can imagine we did not get home particularly early. I took so much stick off of one particular lad at school the following day I lost my head with him in registration as I was tired. I ended up getting a detention for swearing at him and the teacher! Getting time off work is no problem when you are your own boss! I run a small landscaping business.

**The best**

My favourites, well a couple of games where the performances stand out include an away game at Preston where Neil Grayson scored a hat-trick. Preston were doing well in the league and I recall our performances that season were not the best, so to go to Deepdale and win 3-0 and play them off the park was amazing. Cardiff away in the play-off semi-final and 1996-97 was another game. That goal by Sean Parrish was fantastic. I can always remember the weather being rather gloomy and damp until we scored, then the clouds seem to break up and the sun came out! I just had a gut feeling that the Cobblers would go on to win.

Rotherham away in the FA Cup a couple of years back was a fantastic performance. There must have been a good couple of thousand Cobblers supporters there and the support we game the team was immense. Considering the prize at the end of the game (home to Manchester United in the next round of the Cup) and our poor record at Rotherham, this performance and result was something we could only dream of.

Back in the early 90s, I can't remember exactly which season, we had gone on a run of nineteen games without winning before playing Carlisle away. Again, Carlisle were doing well and we were struggling (there seems to be a recurring theme here!) and we went to Brunton Park and won.

One game I always feel very disappointed about is Rochdale away in 1989/90 season. We had beaten Coventry at home in the third round of the FA Cup. Expectations were high when we drawn against Rochdale in the fourth round. At the time we were in a league higher than Rochdale but as usual, the Cobblers did the unexpected and managed to lose 3-0 with a woeful performance. We seem to save some of our worst performances for cup games: Crawley and Canvey Island (both non-league opposition) and then Barnet a couple of seasons ago. That second half performance, when John Gorman was still in charge, was nothing short of embarrassing.

Then, of course, there was going to Scunthorpe and losing 7-0 (in fact, thinking about it, any trip to Scunthorpe is not good). I remember a sequence of seeing something like fifteen goals conceded and none scored in three trips there. Rochdale away on New Year's Day when we lost 6-2 was not good either. The weather wasn't good, it was snowing and the performance didn't exactly lift you spirits."

**The long, winding road**

Getting to Sixfields is an easier task when you live locally, but long trips on a Tuesday night or poor runs of form can really test a fans' enthusiasm. Andy has no qualms about setting off on the road to see the Cobblers though; "There is not an away trip I never want to do. In fact, with the lack of atmosphere at Sixfields sometimes, I would rather play forty-six games away from home each season. Some of the long mid-week trips can be difficult, when getting home late and then up fairly early the next day, but I would never consider not going."

**Crazy, completely crazy**

Of course, following your team isn't always about results on the pitch, it's about the stories and laughs that you have on match days. Andy recalls one long, long day out a few years ago;

"Five of us went to Darlington away on New Year's Eve one year. It was when Peter Morris was in Caretaker/Manager role. We were stopping in Blackpool and had to travel to Darlington on the day of the game. The weather was freezing and it had also been snowing. This doesn't sound too out of the ordinary apart from the fact that, as I was the only one who could drive or had a vehicle, we ended up travelling in my single cab pick-up with a hard top on the rear. So with a mattress and a few cushions, three of them settled down in the back for approximately a 700-mile round trip from Northampton to Darlington via Blackpool! Totally illegal I know! On the map, it doesn't look very far between Blackpool and Darlington, but I can assure you it is. One of the most surreal things I remember on the cross Pennine route on the A66, was that it was snowing fairly heavily. The road must have been close to being closing as I remember only one lane being open and the only other vehicles on the road were one snow-plough and one lorry! Fortunately the pick-up was four-wheel drive and boy did I need it. The three lads in the back took three crates of beer with them for the weekend trip. It was that cold in the back that the three crates were still intact by the time we got back to Northampton! All this effort and the team lost 4-1!"

So when will Andy take a break from the Cobblers? Well it doesn't appear that it will be very soon. He travels to matches with his partner Amanda, who is equally as hardcore a fan when it comes to watching the team in claret and white. Amanda added "We work so hard running a business, going to the football gives us a break from work. We will keep going so long as there is a team to support."

Amanda isn't far behind Andy when it comes to being a Cobblers nut. "I have been supporting the Cobblers since the early 1980s when I used to have a season ticket in the old wooden main stand at the County Ground. I may not have been to as many games as Andy, but I started supporting them before he did! I have been to approximately 550 consecutive games. The last game I missed was mid-January 1998 away at Peterborough in the Leyland DAF Cup. Ironically, my 500th consecutive game was about 3 games after Andy clocked up his 900th. The last home game I missed was at the beginning of the 1993/94 season."

**Story told by Andy Gregg and Amanda Scott**

## More Madness

You've just read the Andy's story of over 900 consecutive first team fixtures, but fellow Cobblers fan Lee Geary isn't far behind. At the end of 2007/08 season, He had clocked up 877 consecutive games out of a total of 1,630 fixtures attended. Bad luck meant that the last first team fixture that Lee missed was in the 1991/92 season when he missed the supporters' bus to an away game by ten minutes, thanks to work.

Lee's love affair began in the early seventies and he attended his first ever game, witnessing Manchester United and George Best's rampage 8-2 at the County Ground.

"I was seven years old and went with my dad and brother Shane, we stood in the cricket side near the Spion Kop."

**Great lengths**

Some people will go to great lengths to ensure they are at the match, even the planning of your own wedding. "The biggest length that I have been too to not miss a match was my wedding, Trish and I decided to get married only it could not be a Saturday because of footy, we decided to get married without telling anyone so took the kids, Nick and Jason off to Horsham for a couple of days in the school holidays, met a couple of mates Eva and Kev who helped set everything up and we returned for the home match on the Saturday to watch the Grimsby match and let everyone know we got married."

**The collector**

Lee is obsessed with Northampton Town that much that he claims, "I don't intend to ever miss a Cobblers game, it is my life, I collect the programmes and have sixteen missing from 1970 to 1979, I am still looking for these to complete my collection, I log every game and the goal scorers. There was one match that I didn't want to go to and that was the Shrewsbury away game 1993, as we had to win to stay up, it was the last game of the season, we did win 3-2 after being 2-0 down. I'm not too fond of going to Carlisle away as it is too far especially midweek.

Loads of people think I am mad because I won't miss a match, my boss knows I support the Cobblers so at the start of the season I give him the fixtures list and the dates I need to take as holidays for midweek games.

I have a good memory of games and my top memories are moving to Sixfields and going to Wembley twice (of course). My best match was beating Bristol City 7-1 at the County Ground, this was on Sunday September 19th, 1982 and the worst was away at Scunthorpe on Saturday October 16th, 1993 where we lost 7-0."

**A long trip to the bog**

"I will go to great lengths to make sure I get to the match. Once I was working night shift and wanted to go to Darlington on a Tuesday night so got my mate to pick me up outside work, told the other workers I was popping to the loo and then came back hours later.

I have had so many good times following the Cobblers, with many friends, some many stories to tell, so many good times, I love following the Cobblers home and away, the family are all season ticket holders and Jason was nine months old when he went to his first match away at Torquay, we won 2-1 and he slept through the whole match. It is certainly a big part of my life."

**Story told by Lee Geary**

*Lee enjoys a pint whilst following the Cobblers' pre-season tour to Seville. Picture sent in by Ian Townsend, also in the photo.*

## Being a Cobblers Supporter from a Disabled Perspective

Home or away, match day is one that I look forward to every week. Along with thousands of other Cobblers supporters. We all take certain things for granted though including walking up the stairs to our seats when we get to the ground, being able to get to the food kiosk at half time, standing up when the mighty Cobblers are on the break and running on the pitch for the end of season celebrations.

**Broom cupboard convenience**

Dedicated Cobblers supporters follow their team through thick and thin but have you ever stopped for a second to think about the large number of disabled supporters the Cobblers have? I for one am wheel chair bound which means I can't walk and have to rely on my wheelchair to get around. Luckily, Sixfields has been fully designed to meet disabled supporters needs but lots of away grounds are to be desired. In some instances, myself and my brother have to sit in front of home fans to cheer on the Claret and Whites because they don't cater for away disabled fans: Port Vale and Tranmere are two grounds that are classic examples of this. Some of the food kiosks are pretty high up so I can't reach them whilst sitting in my chair. Some do not even have disabled parking bays such as Luton Town which means I have to find a place to park away from the ground and push for up to half a mile before and after the game to get to and from my car. It has also been known that some disabled toilets also double up as broom cupboards that are full of mops and brushes.

**Ramp it up**

Lots of these things seem pretty trivial to the everyday supporter and I for one do not wish to be known as a moaner but with all the money in football these days, the FA should be able to go so much further to cater for disabled supporters. We're not talking major changes to make things work. Take Kenilworth Road for instance. All they have to do is take out two concrete steps and provide a concrete ramp and hey presto, I can sit in the same end as the Cobblers supporters. However, none of these things will ever change my mind about following the Cobblers but if ever you fancy a challenge, then feel free to borrow one of my spare chairs to attend a game and see for yourself.

Just one last thought though. If ever you see a disabled car parking bay that is not being used, then think twice before you park in it. They are extra wide for a reason and that's so supporters such as myself can get in and out of my wheel chair when getting in and out of the car.

**Darren Coote**

*Darren with Brothers Gary and Mark*

# Chapter 6 - Funny Old Game

*"It's a funny ol' game Saint!"* I used to love the Saint & Greavsie show in the eighties. It was a light-hearted look at football, sometimes focussing on the fun side of the game. Similar shows like *Fantasy Football* and *Soccer AM* have since arrived on the scene. I love that moment when you're in the pub, reminiscing about the time when lost your contact lens in a goal celebration, only to find it on the way back up the terrace. Seriously, that happened to my mate on the Hotel End once.

The terrace crack is the best, songs like "You're supposed to be a gnome" sung at little Danny Jackson by the Millwall fans. Other great songs include ""Can you tell us if we score?" sung by Cobblers fans to the Brighton fans as the away end was so far from the closest goal, never mind the one we were shooting towards at the other end.

"Mauled by the Tigers, you've been Mauled by the Tigers", with the dangerous mauling type hand gestures and everything, was sung by the Hull fans at Sixfields a few seasons ago. It certainly added to the humour of Cobblers fans who were witnessing a 5-1 home defeat at the time.

Talking of defeats, in a 5-2 reverse at Portsmouth, down to ten men, Town fans started singing, "2-1 we're gonna win 2-1" at 1-0 down
"3-2 we're gonna win 3-2" at 2-0 down

"4-3 we're gonna win 4-3" at 3-1 down

"5-4 we're gonna win 5-4" at 4-2 down

"6-5 we're gonna win 6-5" at 5-2 down. You get the idea? Simple but funny at the time. The funny moments are what make football, I mean sometimes you have to make up for the awful performance and a long away trip on a cold February evening. Here is a collection of a few terrace ticklers, so to speak and a few alternative stories to keep you going...

# Remember That Time at The Cobblers When...

Every Cobblers fan can pick out their best memories from footballing times at Sixfields over the years. Moving to what was a world away from the ramshackle uniqueness of the quaint County Ground in 1994, to a sharp newly concreted stadium, the level of football and standard the club have set themselves could only improve, but there are still moments down the years that make you ponder, smile, laugh, cry, angry, focused and downright happy. That is why I felt it was important to capture a few of the moments that supporters are bound to ramble about for years to come, starting with the sentence, "Do you remember that time at Cobblers when..."

**Wait for it**

Sixfields first game was scheduled for the beginning of the 1994/95 season, even had a *last ever game* versus Chester City with a special programme to boot but after months of delays the new clean-cut stadium unveiled to the public on 15th October 1994 when Northampton faced Barnet. And a day for the late Martin Aldridge, producing arguably the best forward somersault celebration after becoming the first Cobbler to score in front of the new North Stand.

**Hole-y cow**

When Sixfields used to be publicly branded a community stadium, American Football and Rugby League was on the cards. Those different combination of sports left its mark when Northampton faced Fulham in Sixfields' third ever game, November 1994. Visiting goalkeeper Jim Stannard saw practice come to an abrupt halt when a huge crater appeared in the Fulham goalmouth, his leg half encased in a huge hole, prompting some urgent action from ground staff and delaying the match by ten minutes. Rugby posts were to blame so best that Town and Saints stay well clear then!

**Oh what fun it is to see Orient win away... twice**

One club who beam radiantly when *Sixfields* and *mid 1990's away wins* are mentioned in the same sentence were Leyton Orient. In September 1995, Orient made their 43rd consecutive away League trip, this time to Sixfields. Having not won on their travels since September 1993, at 1-1 it looked like another winless effort. Until Alex Inglethorpe popped up with a 93rd minute winner that is! Delirious O's fans flooded the pitch like they'd just won promotion, definitely a sight to behold. Orient then went on another barren run without an away League win, until exactly one year later. The same Tuesday night at Sixfields, Daniel Chapman netted during injury time, sealing another famous victory. No wonder Barry Hearn was quoted at the time: "If this isn't heaven, then I must be in Northampton." How true!

**Thank heavens for that**

The Sixfields pitch received another real test of strength on the visit of Doncaster in Division Three action in February 1996. Literally an hour before kick-off, the heavens opened to leave the pitch sodden. Referee John Brandwood's task of letting the game go ahead was stretched to the limit, frantic forking (yes, forking) ensued by worried ground staff and a kick-off was then agreed. Just as well, a superb, if not very sodden, 90 minutes ended with Jason White slotting home a last-minute penalty in the 3-3 ding dong battle. Fantastic Sixfields football.

**Griffin 'ell**

One thing you do as a club mascot is show yourself up. *Griff the Griffin* was a strange mascot choice, apparently is a "legendary creature with the body of a lion and the head and wings of an eagle. More like an oversized magnolia baby chick. The Griffin surprisingly chose a damp FA Cup First Round 1-day vs Hayes, to lead the team out by sprinting full pelt out of the tunnel, thirty yards onto the pitch, turn towards the West Stand waving frantically and whoops, slip aerially upwards flat onto his back. Cue roaring laughter from four sides of the ground as the Griff *flapped* around trying to atone for the horrendous error, whilst players trudged past offering no help to this clown. No wonder he was soon replaced with Clarence the Dragon.

**The month of smiles and goals**

Some fans will remember Neil Grayson dive bomb head first into the snow after netting the fourth goal in a 4-0 v. Cardiff, a fixture played in minus temperatures on New Year's Day 1997. In fact, the club made a heartfelt plea to clearly hungover supporters to help clear the pitch of heavy snow, bringing spades, shovels, wheelbarrows, and mountains of dedication.

Indeed, Town were restricted to just three games in January 1997 due to adverse weather. That didn't matter, fans were treated to twelve goals in just three matches, including Neil Grayson's four-minute hat-trick vs Hartlepool, and a 5-1 win over Chester thanks to loanee Matthew Rush's running the show, all in the club's centenary and promotion year!

**Horse play in the semi**

Does anyone remember the happenings outside on the North Stand hill of the Play-Off semi-final vs Cardiff in 1997? A memory of watching from the West Stand went something like this:

Northampton fans cheering on the hill outside the North Stand towards the game's conclusion

Cardiff fans (obviously out the stadium early) chase Northampton fans up and around the hill

Police horses chase Cardiff fans up and around the hill

Cardiff fans turn and chase the horses back towards the West Stand!

Nothing short of a Benny Hill sketch! (read the above again whilst singing the theme... du-du-du dur dur duddle-luddle lur dur duddle-luddle du dur-dur du-duddle lur...)

**Handbags... handbags**

David Moyes and Ian Atkins are two character managers with passion for management boiling through their veins. None so much when Town hosted Preston North End in October 1998. James Hunt secured a last gasp equaliser to earn a 1-1 draw. At the final whistle, shaking hands quickly turned into shaking fists with a few strong words exchanged inside the centre circle, and suddenly a 22 man brawl erupted in front of the dugouts. Atkins unbelievably launched at Moyes, grabbing the now Everton manager by the throat as a few roundhouses and headlocks resumed. Amazingly, Atkins dismissed the clear level of vitriol between the teams with a bizarre quote on Anglia News post-match, stating "It was only a bit of handbags" and "It was nothing more than a push or a shove." He never did talk things up, except our first *'£1million'* striker Chris Lee.

**Cobblers "Seal" victory, eventually**

One ridiculous moment in FA Cup action saw the quickest Sixfields sending-off ever seen! Striker David Seal was red carded after barely two minutes versus Lancaster City in November 1998. After jumping into a defender on the opposing goal-line, words were exchanged with stopper Mark Thornley, who he then appeared to slyly kick. Barely believing the stupidity of the Australian striker, referee Andy D'Urso was left with no option but to brandish the red! Cobblers avoided the giant-killing despite going one behind to Peter Thomson's strike. But the Lancaster forward netted again... this time with a headed own goal on 55 minutes, then Ian Sampson barely a minute later to *seal* their passage to Round Two.

**Suuuuper Su-per John**
John Gayle was known for his bullish style (well, he's hardly the most graceful of players) and displayed this trait with a tackle that would see him banned for a good few matches. Against Walsall in December 1998, keeper James Walker slid out to collect a low cross, without banking on Gayle launching a wild two footed tackle on his head! A lengthy delay for treatment and eventual substitution to the groggy goalie, midfielder Mark Blake went between the sticks and amazingly eleven minutes of injury time had to be added on before half time could be taken! This was the days when sub card was held up, I don't think the 4th official had two 1's! Cobblers won the encounter 3-2.

**Anyone else wanna join him...? Anyone?**
Most will remember the ridiculous game that witnessed a 3-0 League win v Torquay in October 1999. The Gulls somehow played the final 15 minutes with only EIGHT men and somehow only conceded two goals. Brian Healy saw a second booking after just seventeen minutes, and at 1-0, Lee Russell followed on seventy-five minutes for a rash challenge earning him his second yellow. Torquay players snapped at referee Michael Ryan and he immediately brandished a red card to Robbie Herrara in the ensuing chaos, clearly incensed by his decision. Tony Battersby and Ian Sampson rounded off proceedings with goals, but ageing goalkeeper Neville Southall - still playing at forty-one years of age, rolled back the years to halt Cobblers from making double figures with brilliant saves.

**Swansea – Match Postponed**
It's not often that matches get postponed at Sixfields, it's the kind of ground which escapes most harsh elements despite having its fair share of torrential weather thrown at the turf, and the number of cancellations

due to adverse conditions is probably less than once a year on average since 1994. Though during the 2000-01 season, the club actually struggled to get Swansea City home game underway! Firstly, the September date was postponed due to the Swans' international involvements. Moved to mid-December, it then fell afoul of particularly wet weather and a waterlogged pitch put paid to any game. The club rescheduled for late January and were gobsmacked when more rain saw most of the pitch covered in water. Initially given a date for a week in early February, the club settled on a late February date. It's just as well for all the postponements, the exotically named Frenchman Fabiano had put the visitors 1-0 up before half time, any hope looked lost until Ian Sampson pulled back an eighty-ninth minute equaliser. Then Marco Gabbiadini sent Sixfields wild by bagging a 90th minute winner!

**Town Sponsor Hudds Cancellation**

Sixfields has certainly seen some harsh weather conditions over the years. In March 2003, howling winds was making conditions difficult in the game versus Huddersfield. Marc Richards had put Town 1-0 ahead early on, but no-one could have foreseen the problems with flying sponsor boards unhinged by the gusts - one of which injured a Terriers' supporter in the South Stand (treated at the scene). Meanwhile panic ensued when another board was ripped off the East Stand and flew luckily sideways across the stand towards the South Stand toilets. Police immediately intervened and consulted with match referee Nigel Miller at pitch side, before making the reluctant decision to halt proceedings on 36 minutes. Unfortunately, the replayed match saw Northampton lose 1-0 in a corking game, with future Cobblers 'keeper Paul Rachubka on top form.

**Ref looks at his watch and blows up...early**

Referee Ray Olivier is known for getting Cobblers fans backs up on more than one occasion over the seasons, none so much for this inexplicable mistake on Valentine's Day 2004. Unbelievably, as a long clearance was played after forty-four minutes, Olivier blew up for half-time, despite the stadium clock showing 35 seconds left of normal time! Confused fans pointed to the clock (as well as checking their watches did state 3:44pm), whilst baffled players and management from Northampton, losing 1-0 at the time, rushed towards the official to point out the obvious mistake.

Even though three players received treatment during the half, no injury time board had yet gone up and Olivier left the field to shout and jeers as he refused to sanction what should have been at least three minutes more. No harm done; Cobblers went on to win 3-1! In the same match, loan striker Magno Vieira scored his first goal for the club His wild celebrations were fantastic, only stalled by a ridiculous comedy moment where he was struck with cramp, left rooted firmly to the spot and a strange stance. People thought he was about to keel over, poor lad!

**Not the Smart-est thing to say**
One-time Cobblers loanee Alan Smart certainly gave the younger generation a new word to take to school on Monday, when he was disgracefully sent off on 65 minutes of the Northampton vs Bury game in September 2005 - while his team were 1-0 up! His outburst was fuelled by a foot-up challenge from a Northampton player, worthy of a possible booking in itself, and decided the time was right to use the "C" word - twice! Gasps of amazement came from home fans, referee Darren Deadman pausing only to get the nod from the offended linesman before an instant red. What made it worse? Smart was appearing his first game back after a three-match ban for another sending-off!

**Live Orr learn**
Bradley Orr's extraordinary red card cast a big shadow over ten-man Bristol City's gutsy 3-1 win over Northampton Town during a televised Sky Sports game in August 2006, where referee Michael Jones had no choice but to brandish the punishment after two team mates were involved in a mindless scuffle seconds before the break. The debacle began when Robins' pair Louis Carey and Orr traded insults, head butts and almost blows in an argument after an unmarked Andy Kirk's shot was superbly saved by Adriano Basso at his near post. The pair had to be separated, but Mr Jones decided that Orr was the aggressor of the disagreement and sent him off. Ironically, just a week after the incident, Orr and team-mate Steve Brooker were jailed for 28 days following their part in a nightclub brawl nearly a year earlier.

**Starlings induce Northampton strike**
Boxing Day 2006, the Christmas turkey devoured and it's back to Sixfields. Fans had started noticing another type of bird flocking around the ground

on a regular basis - a murmuration of starlings. In the dull moments during Town games, it's usually a calming pleasure to watch the birds flighting formations out over the South East corner and produce fancy darting shapes before they roosted. Now, the question was posed whether something more sinister was occurring! Narrowly prior to Town netting their first goal against Cheltenham, a demonstration of an amazing swooping formation took place which some claim brought on Northampton's first home goal.

**Doig is the saviour**

Chris Doig received a rightful standing ovation and drew laughs from a somewhat *Dad's Army* St John's Ambulance crew in the League match v Millwall in December 2006. On a sodden wet pitch, Cobbler-to-be Poul Hubertz put the Lions 1-0 up after eleven minutes. On thirty-four minutes, Millwall full back Danny Senda went down in the North East corner signalling what seemed like a bad injury. Both physios raced from their dugout and St John's "sprung" into action... though were found hopelessly at sixes and sevens. Three proceeded across the pitch slipping and sliding in their shiny shoes, another forgot the medical bag, so had to return, one stood rooted to the spot amongst the mud, grass and puddles and one gallantly tried to carry on - until a stretcher was signalled! Realising the vital equipment was ambulance bound below the control box (the crowd hooting with laughter at St John's ineptness), skipper Doig lost patience, sprinted 100 yards to and from the ambulance and retrieved the stretcher. Millwall fans rose in unison to applaud the act - which earned Doig the Football League "Good Sport Award" in March 2007. To add to the entertainment, referee Iain Williamson was forced to abandon the game on sixty-eight minutes due to persistent rain making the pitch waterlogged - so the game doesn't officially exist!

**Haha what a stupid *&$***

A typical end of season at Sixfields ends in bitter disappointment or the crack at promotion. Most in 2008 were settling for a decent mid table position, and a good celebration to see off striker Poul Hubertz. Tranmere were the opposition and with what could be described as a lively bunch of fans, really made the day. Ian Goodison's red card on eighty minutes prompted one Scouser to confront the referee on the pitch (immediately hauled out by stewards). But on the final whistle, home supporters did their usual trick of invading the pitch, congratulating players and occasionally giving the goad to the opposition support. Rovers however had other ideas, straying onto the pitch themselves despite a wall of fluorescent jackets keeping them at bay. Until one absolute donkey broke free to run the gauntlet

There are loads of great memories over the years, and many more are still yet untold or even unfolded. But one thing is for sure, Sixfields is never, ever a dull, straightforward place where football is concerned.

Simon Sidwell

## Lethal Weapon

During my forty years of watching the Cobblers I have never known anything as bizarre as the incident that happened to me at Leyton Orient 1st September 2007. I have travelled the length and breadth of the country, visiting many grounds but Orient was something else!

**Handbags at five paces**

Upon entering the ground, the stewards insisting on checking in mine and my mate's handbags. I really hate it when stewards insist on 'just having a look' in my handbag before I go in to a ground. OK, in these days of heightened security I do accept the need for searches, if it's carried out on everyone but do these stewards search men's pockets? No they don't. I suspect they get some kind of perverted kick out of looking in women's handbags, because clearly, they can't be expecting to find anything more dangerous than a girly purse in there. Or so I always thought.

**Baggage check-in**

So, as we arrived at the match, two stewards asked to *just have a look* in my bag. My mate made some comment about how they could never be too careful. She was security cleared and allowed to proceed through the turnstile. Next was my turn for the search and I was devastated that they found the dangerous object in my bag. So dangerous that they had to confiscate it during the match for the protection of other supporters.

Now it is time for a multiple-choice question; was the dangerous object?
a) A Stanley knife
b) A razor blade fixed to the handle of a hair brush
c) A bottle of perfume

Well of course, the answer is C. Yes, in fact when I had pinched myself to check I was not dreaming, these two jobsworths were really telling me that I couldn't go into a football ground in possession of a bottle of perfume. I honestly thought they were joking as did my friend, but then it dawned on me as they were explaining where I would need to collect my dangerous bottle of perfume from after the match that they were seriously telling me they intended to confiscate my bloody perfume. It took me approximately thirty seconds to come to an "Over my dead body" situation. I asked somewhat incredulously if there had ever been a recorded incident of a bottle of perfume being used in anger at a football match. "*Oh yes, it happens at lower league matches you know*", says Jobs Worth Number One. (LOWER LEAGUE MATCHES??? Erh, we weren't clear if that meant our level or lower still). If anyone knows of any such incident do please let me know and I will offer a public apology to Leyton Orient but in the meantime, I intend to say what I think of them.

**The principle of the matter**

Anyway, suddenly not even caring if I have travelled seventy odd miles to go to this match, I found myself saying to my friend "If I can't take the perfume in with me, they aren't getting a penny of my money. We will go home." (Yes sure - as he pointed out later, what we would actually have done was gone back to the car, put the perfume in it and sneaked back to the ground but I digress).

By this time what passes for a crowd of fellow Cobblers supporters were listening to this exchange with disbelief (OK, I think there were two others), which was when I, bizarrely in view of the fact that I never admit to my age, announced to all and sundry "For Christ sake, I am nearly 50. Do you seriously think there is the remotest chance I am going to throw my perfume at anyone?" The damn stuff is bloody expensive for a start! I was too annoyed to notice but my mate says it was at that stage that the stewards started to look vaguely embarrassed and did in fact bend the rules to allow me into the ground in possession of a bottle of perfume. I was very glad we did go in as I would have hated to have missed what really was a great game of football which ended 2-2.

**The referee's a ...**

But I tell you what. The referee was so bloody awful that had my aim been any better, he would have found himself floored by a bottle of Chanel No 5! In fairness I should add I was so p*ssed off by what had happened that I wrote to Orient, and got a very apologetic email back the very next day. Just a quick one for you. I won't bore you for too long. Here's my contribution to the book.

Having been present at Cobblers matches for nearly fifteen years despite only turning twenty in early 2008, I already find myself wondering where all the years have gone. I'm lucky to have been born and bred into this football club at an interesting period in our history which seems to consistently throw some trial or tribulation up for us to be entertained by. Whereas many of my fellow supporters would name their best moments as Pat Gavin skillfully using his backside at Gay Meadow or THAT swing of John Frain's left boot. I would class one of my own as the eight-hour round trip to see Paul Trollope salvage us an 87th minute draw at Carlisle in 2004 alongside 196 other Cobblers. Whilst it might not sound at all glamorous, it sticks out in my memory because of the circumstances surrounding the trip. At the time I was only 16 and in the middle of the run up to my GCSE's, which meant having MOCK practice papers in the middle of March. Around the same time as our trip to Brunton Park actually. I normally wouldn't have travelled but at that time it looked extremely likely that Carlisle would be relegated that year. Not wanting to pass up the opportunity to 'tick another one off the 92' as to speak we left Northampton at about 2pm, right around the same time as my Mock History exam started.

It was worth the trip just for the point, even if I ended up with an absolute rollocking at school on the Wednesday morning.

Jane Smith

# The Collector

Trawling around a car boot sale early on a Sunday morning might not seem to be everyone's idea of fun, but when it comes to a programme collector, it can be a goldmine.

**Money for old rope**

For in the days when as a kid, I, as well as hundreds of others, were taken to The Cobblers to watch a game and come home clutching a match programme. Never in a million years did anyone expect those scrappy pieces of paper become so collectable and valuable in modern times. In fact, the phrase "*If I knew then, what I knew now*" has been heard many a time by collectors at programme fairs as they walk around and see the prices of yesteryears relics.

Like many, programme collecting started as a schoolboy hobby with the likes of Steve Earl and Dick Rattray popular names in the playground. Nowadays it is a multimillion-pound business with websites, auctions, fairs etc., with some programmes fetching several hundreds of pounds. All Cobblers programme collectors hope one day, to have a copy of every single programme available from the nineteenth century to last week's match, but as we all know, this is nothing but a distant dream.

**Same old, same old**

The concept of the football programme has basically remained the same for well over a hundred years, it is an informative article relating to the forthcoming match with players names, statistics, news, views and an insight into the opposition.

**Marketing and advertising**

Advertising has always been popular way of raising club funds and has slowly evolved from *Bill Bloggs* the local baker, and adverts to get your shoes re-soled to more recently the multi-national companies. A good percentage of old programmes have the scores written on them or notes inside as years ago before televisions and computers this was the only real way of collating scores and statistics. Initially, Cobblers programmes were issued as a single sheet with the very basic of information, and gradually through the decades have grown in quality and quantity.

## The quest

The Holy Grail for most Cobblers collectors must be to own a copy of the 1908 Charity Shield against Newcastle United, but for most, to own programmes from the early 1960's onwards seems more realistic.

Programmes from the late fifties were made of shiny but very thin paper, and a few years later were halved in size to fit into supporters' pockets.

The famous year of 1965/6 is still highly collectable as it is a keepsake of our finest hour and when a single copy or a whole season are offered for sale, they can change hands at very high prices (£500+). The highlight of this season is to own a copy of the Blackburn away League Cup programme. As this was a single sheet programme and was attended by just a few thousand fans, it was probably made scarcer by the fact that The Cobblers actually won on a cold wet night, hence most Rovers fans probably throwing away their copy in disgust.

## That famous FA Cup tie again

A George Best double hat-trick Man United in their 8-2 win in February 1970 is good enough reason for hardened United and Cobblers fans alike to hoard a copy of this match programme. This often changes hands for around £50 even though George's name was never down on the team sheet to play that day.

## Environmental issues

In the 1973/4 season, the football programme took a setback as an indirect result of the Power Strike, the production of our programme was cut back to a single sheet issue in an effort to conserve waste.

The opposite in fact seemed to happen in the 1979/80 season when the normal A5 sized issue was replaced by a trendy A3 sized newspaper style programme but with poor quality paper. Other teams produced the same style programme that year, but common sense prevailed and they all resorted back the common size the following season.

## Sabbath day

The 1982/3 season saw the first ever Cobblers game on a Sunday. At the time it was against the law to pay admission to see a match on the Sabbath, to get around this, the admission price was charged to *'buy'* the programme and technically to see the game was free.

## Dark days

The dark era of the McRitchie campaign never escaped controversy, because with money being virtually none existent, our existing programme printers were not paid, and they refused to print anymore, so it was only through the hard work of a Cobblers fan (Rob Marshall) that two programmes were printed in order that the club met with Football League rules. The first being a single sheet typed photocopy against Burnley, and then a *'fanzine'* type programme against Scarborough.

## Shiny and mass produced

So to this day, full glossy magazines are produced in which The Cobblers have excelled and won a few awards. But at £2.50 to £3 per issue, a collector will have to splash out well over £150 a season to keep up with times, which brings me back to Sunday mornings walking around a grassy field hoping to find some 'rubbishy old football things' thrown in an old shoe box and bought for just pence each ...with the hope that maybe just one day...

**Andy Trasler**

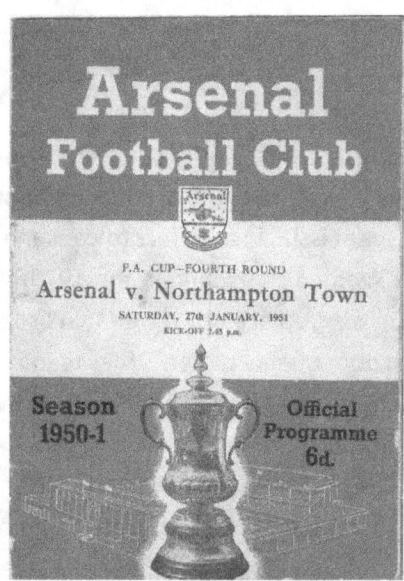

*Rare as.... a collectable programme from the Cobblers visit to Arsenal for the FA Cup fourth round tie in 1951. This was sent in by Tony Lyon.*

# Five Obscure Alternatives to Wembley

**09/09/1977 Southport 3-1 Cobblers (Robertson)**

I was a young, naïve and solitary Cobblers fan sat between my mum and dad in the main home stand. The Cobblers weren't really in it and Southport were stroking the ball around the back four. It all got too much for me so I stood up and shouted, "C'mon you chickens!" A chorus of clucking noises echoed around the stand and Mum told me to sit down...probably because I was obscuring her view of Southport playboy Eric Snookes. The one and only time I've been heckled by opposing fans.

**08/01/1983 Cobblers 0-1 Aston Villa**

I didn't go to this game but took great pleasure in telling all my Gillingham supporting school friends that the Cobblers would be on Match of the Day at the weekend, having beaten the Gills to reach the third round of the FA Cup. Apart from the marvellous Steve Massey my outstanding memory of this game was watching Peter Coffill try and flick the ball up with the back of his heel while the game had stopped for a foul. It was a poor decision by Peter in front of a nationwide audience.

**26/04/1986 Cobblers 0-2 Cambridge Utd**

This was the last Saturday home game of the season prior to the all-conquering Championship season. We didn't turn up that day but I remember meeting up with friends later that evening at the Churchill's pub in Chatham full of hope and optimism - not that any of them were remotely interested. Never in my wildest dreams did I think we would achieve what we did in that following season.

**01/09/1990 Maidstone Utd 1-3 Cobblers (Wilson, Wood, Thorpe)**

Why I went to a game with a bag of grapes remains a mystery. I wasn't ill or there being national sympathy for grape growers. I don't remember the game at all but I do remember a giant of a man eating my grapes without my permission. I was casually eating the aforementioned grapes when all of a sudden, we scored. In the mayhem I had lost my healthy snack. I was searching the immediate terracing when I turned around and saw a Shirley Crabtree looky-likey scoffing my five-a-day. I pretended they were nothing to do with me and returned later with a meat pie.

**13/01/2004 Rotherham Utd 1-2 Cobblers (Walker, Smith)**
The original tie should have been won by Derek Asamoah but in reality, it was a game that sparked little interest in either Northampton or Rotherham, until the fourth-round draw was made. The replay at Rotherham was electric. I personally was fired up not by the lure of Man Utd but by the smug and misguided confidence of the Chuckle Brothers. This game was one of those rare magical away days with everything at stake.

**Paul Hardman aka auntie**

---

## My Top 3 Northampton Moments

10-year-old Christian Hardman tells us his top three Cobblers moments from supporting Northampton from his home in Bolton.

*The lucky mascot leads his team of heroes out at the Kassam Stadium. Christian looks even more focussed than Chris Willmott!*

**1. Oxford 1-2 Northampton** I will remember this game for the rest of my life as I was the Cobblers lucky mascot. I can remember getting a bunch of sweets off Colin Calderwood that kept on falling out of my pocket! I sat next to the players in the dressing room and trained with the subs. I never actually sat in the dug-out during the game but I went into the stand with my dad.

**2. Northampton 1-0 Chester** this was the very game that got us promoted from League Two. I ran onto the pitch after the game and got on my dad's shoulders to see The Town set off a bottle of champagne!

**3. 2007/08 Sponsors Evening** A memory that I will never forget. My dad was the home kit sponsor of Giles Coke. Giles took me round and got all the players to sign my shirt. I was on his and Chris Doig's table and had a nice chat. The food was great and I got to show my top at school the next day.

## Greatest Day of Our Lives

**Rags to riches**

From the lowest attendance in the Third Division on a cold, wet night in deepest Doncaster in November to sipping champagne en-route to the most famous stadium in the whole world, Wembley. What a season!

Our day started when we all met up for face painting, hair colouring and of course, a photo call. Sixfields Boys was blasting from the radio and neighbours couldn't help but look at this claret and white clad bunch. Our furry friend, mascot Oscar, wasn't risked as he hadn't been too popular on away trips this season, his last trip was a defeat at struggling Brighton. Soon we were off down the M1, flags flying, ribbons on aerials, horns blasting, what sights and sounds. Our first sights of the brown Wembley signs and we can't believe that it's Northampton Town who will be playing there. But it's for real! If we needed proof, we got it walking up Wembley Way amid a sea of claret and white spotting the magic words between the twin towers read Northampton Town. Pinch me this is a dream!

We take our seats and the places starts to fill up. The Cobblers players are on the pitch taking in the atmosphere. At the other end you can still read 'Wembley' in the seats, which are sparsely populated by Swansea fans.

Then the proudest moment as Ian Atkins leads the team out to an amazing reception of tickertape, flags waving, cheering and shouting, it was magnificent! Our group were too tense to really enjoy the match, fearing extra time in the end. Obviously, it wasn't to be, John Frain had other ideas and you know the rest.

This was undoubtedly the greatest day of our lives and something to cherish forever. We owe it all to Ian Atkins and the team for a fabulous day out.

**...and a word from the bear**

I am now a bare bear. Yes, they even took my shirt to Wembley with them but left me at home in my shorts and cap. Things started to go wrong for me in November 1996 at Darlington when I got blamed for the result.

I was retired but managed to persuade them to take me to Brighton, where I had my photo taken in my own seat in the stand. Everyone was polite to me until the ninety minutes were up, then I had to go home by car as I feared for my life on the coach.

Back to Wembley. I didn't want to spoil their fun so I posed for the photo in the morning and then wished them all the best. They had clocked up hundreds of miles supporting the lads. They left the radio on for me to listen to the match and began to think that I wasn't the jinx but I fell off my chair when Frainy scored in injury time. Oh how I wish I'd have been there, but they did show me the video afterwards, playing the song and talking about it for hours on end about the best day of their lives.

**Cheryl Byrne**

*Lee Wade captures the greatest moment of a Cobblers fans' life. John Frain's free kick flies into the net beneath the twin towers.*

# Stand Up If You Hate The P*sh

Trips to Northampton are great. There are many reasons for this, most notable being the fact that we always win. Always - even when we're rubbish. Ian Ashbee used to score once every three seasons for us, and we've scored less direct free kicks in our time than any team you've ever known, but even he managed a magnificent thirty yarder at Sixfields back in John Beck's second spell in charge.

Better than that was a great game the season before everything fell apart for the U's and we fell out of the league, when under the leadership of the legendary John Taylor, one of the youngest U's sides ever to take to the field secured a great 2-1 win with a last minute goal from Adam Tann, memorably compared to Claude Makelele in the week leading up to the game by Taylor. He was wrong of course; Claude never scores such a sweet finish as Tann managed that night.

Of course, the one thing that unites both clubs is a fondness for a bit of banter around that lot up the road and their rotund general manager, the inimitable Mr Fry. Even as Ashbee's thirty yarder crashed into the net, the strains from all four sides imploring Mr Fry to cheer up about the poor state of his cherished club were just fading away.

Sixfields is also renowned for being difficult to park in. Every time I go it appears that there is a new sign up forbidding parking in another section of the *leisure complex* parking site, meaning you have to walk further down the grassy slope to the ground, always quicker on your backside as I found to my cost one particularly wet night.

In all seriousness, what really stands out as a memory for me is in United's darkest hour, desperately staving off relegation, some shocking business decisions by the then board and with a rubbish team looking down the barrel of relegation, it was Northampton Town fans and stewards who offered to stand outside their grounds shaking the buckets. It was Cobblers fans who donated change and in many cases more. It was Northampton fans that shook our hands and wished us luck. And of course, the Northampton players that let Adam Tann get that memorable winner. Thanks for the memories, see you on the other side.

**Ben Yelton (Cambridge United Fan)**

# Big Exile

**A long, long way**

Getting to watch the Cobblers regularly is pretty difficult for me these days. That is because I have the long trip from Qatar to get to home games, but here is a short story of my time back in UK. I have been a Cobblers fan for many years since going to watch Northampton beat Cambridge back at the old County Ground fifteen or so years ago.

**Pick and mix**

More recently however, I had taken my girlfriend Denise and son Oliver to watch their first ever football match. We started off by a trip to the cinema to watch the film *Jumper*, although my mind wasn't on the film as I was really excited at the prospect of watching us attempting to beat Swansea. I was feeling pretty confident, as I do every week and felt that, despite their superiority at the top of the league table, on our day, we were a match for anyone in that league. Plus, with my working overseas in Middle East, I don't get to watch my team as much as I would like to.

We watched the game and after visiting the club shop, we had some of fun. Oliver enjoying getting his photos taken with Clarence. The girlfriend, like a lot of her gender compatriots, wasn't too convinced at going to a football match and within minutes of getting inside the stadium, she had miraculously transformed from an egg-chasing Saints fan into a Cobblers hooligan (well maybe I have exaggerated somewhat) but the transformation was there to see. She was singing along with the crowd and clapping throughout the match. The boy was also joining in with the singing along.

The game itself was a great contest and we were leading 3-1 at half-time and could have been beating them by seven - the final score was 4-2, the same score line between the same teams 30 or 40 years previously. This previous match was shown in the match day programme from that day.

Afterwards, the boy was so excited at his first football match that he was singing the words "Top of the league, you're having a laugh" and got told off for singing "who's a diving b*stard?" I honestly to this day, don't know who that came from!

**Paul Coates (living on Doha, Qatar)**

# More Than Ten Years On

It has been over ten years since fans have shared these memories and they were first published in print and I hope you enjoyed them.

A lot has changed at Northampton and clubs around the country. Some of the younger fans who shared their memories in this book will now have grown up, become adults and sadly we've lost a few older fans too.

The Cobblers have had a number of managers and players come and go since too. We have beaten top flight teams including Liverpool at Anfield, been to Wembley again (although one to forget), almost gone out of business and romped away with the league title under Chris Wilder. The rollercoaster continues and new memories are forged.

**Back to the future**

The modern day Cobblers have moved a million miles from the days at the run down County Ground. We have moved into the corporate market that football has become in the days of Marketing Managers and Prawn Sandwiches (although I have never ever actually seen someone eating seafood at a football match that goes beyond fish and chips). Parts of me want Northampton Town to remain a small club and keep the personal level, but the only way forward is investment, ground development and a 24 hour operation, so there is no point dwelling in the past.

**Playing for your club**

Many youngsters dream of playing for their club, they pretend to be their favourite players in the playground and act out goals whilst dreaming they have just won the cup or something. I like millions of other kids did this in my school days, my dream was playing for the Cobblers and winning the FA Cup with them. Now I'm a few years older and probably, questionably a few wiser too, I know the likelihood of both happening have become somewhat longer odds than they days of the school yard, but I had the joy of pulling on the claret shirt and representing my club on a number of occasions. Towards the end of the 2002/03 season, I started playing for the Cobblers Fans Team and despite losing to Hull City Coasters 6-0, I really enjoyed the banter between the two sets of fans.

That game was a new beginning for me in my love affair of Northampton Town Football Club. Suddenly I felt an even bigger part of the club that I had supported all of my life.

My first game as team organiser was a July fixture against Hull City Coasters again. One of their lads was on a stag weekend, white water rafting at the Nene Centre on the Bedford Road and they got in touch to see if we could accommodate a game. Just as the professionals do, I'm sure, I was a little nervous as I drove to the pitch at Moulton College. Would my directions for our players be good enough? Would our lads meet them in time to escort them to this hard to find pitch (for a non-local)? Would everyone turn up? Would the new players enjoy it? But everything went smoothly and we kicked off in good time.

Now to have a fairy tale start to my new role in the team, I couldn't have asked for one much better. With the game only two minutes old, I tried a speculative shot from 30 yards. I didn't catch it right, but the keeper fluffed his save at the near post and the ball squeezed into the net. It was my first fans team goal and for those who know my footballing ability, they will tell you that I don't get many.

There were so many highlights playing fans team foot including our 5-5 draw with Leicester's Internet Foxes in 2008. It was featured on Sky Sports when I presented "My Big League Weekend" on the Monday night goals round up show. They couldn't have picked a better game to watch!

It was an honour to play against Ian Sampson, Ray Warburton, Sean Parrish and Eddie McGoldrick on a few occasions at Sixfields in end of season charity matches.

I played up until 2012 when I forced to stop contact sports following a head injury so my last 11 a side game was actually at Sixfields, I suppose you could say it was a good way to bow out of football.

**Behind the scenes**

It was a great experience to work behind the scenes on a few occasions. Firstly, the company I spent many years at, Starting Off, sponsored the Youth Team. This gave me another insight to the club and made me realise the hard work and dedication that these youngsters have to put into *making it* as they say.

Having never been a great footballer myself, it angers me to see a player throw away their big chance by hitting the bottle or letting it all go to their heads, so the discipline that is instilled into them by those in charge.

A few years after, we piloted a sports nutrition project in my business and worked with the youth and first team, meeting players including Bayo Akinfenwa, Chris Doig, Clarke Carlisle and the rest of the squad plus manager Aidy Boothroyd. Advising players was a real great experience and realising that they are decent chaps who lead everyday lives.

**Trust the editor**

Not many fans around the country are aware of the fact the whole supporters trust movements started at Northampton. If it had been anywhere a little more famous, it would probably be branded all over everything, but because it was an unfashionable, lowly team that nobody really cared about, we probably miss a little bit of the recognition at times. Over a few seasons I helped out at a good number of NTFC Supporters Ltd (the Trust of today) events, but one thing that stuck in my mind was when Sixfields was the venue for a regional Supporters Direct meeting. A Notts County fan was present and he was delighted to be inside the Sixfields complex and told me how honoured he was to be at the ground where it all began. I hadn't the heart to tell him that we had moved grounds since it all began.

Another significant moment in my Cobblers supporting history came in the 2004/05 season. Along came the birth of HotelEnders, the new Cobblers fanzine. For many years I had enjoyed the musings of Rob Marshall's 'What A Load Of Cobblers', but Rob hung up his pen due to work commitments.

It certainly has been a great time since the day the first issue was churned out on a cheap black and white laser printer. Our house used to be full of fanzine pages in the week leading up to a new issue, until we decided to get them printed at a printers. The aim was to maintain the tradition of a black and white retro style magazine in order to preserve some of football's history.

Finally thank you to everyone who has contributed to this book all those years ago and we hope you enjoy these memories that are etched into history.

## Thank You to Our Contributors

| | | |
|---|---|---|
| George Phipps | Tony Lyon | Dave Blake |
| Derrick Thompson | Frank Grande | Steve Riches |
| Patrick Kennedy | Nigel Wheatley | Mike Hermann |
| Andy Trasler | John Atkinson | Stuart Bailey |
| Jack Berry (Bury) | Paul Hardman | Martin Wade |
| Lee Wade | Tom Reed | Norman Nickason |
| Bob Duff | Roger Averill | Ian Townend |
| Jules Kennedy | Steve Ward | Dan Brothers |
| Sean Revill (Mansfield) | Glen Cousner | Sean Wilkinson |
| James Averill | Luis Pereira | Chris Evans |
| Katy Kennedy | Orin Willis | Bobby the Cobbler |
| Ben Trasler | Andy Gregg | Amanda Scott |
| Lee Geary | Darren Coote | Simon Sidwell |
| Jane Smith | Christian Hardman | Cheryl Byrne |
| Ben Yelton (Cambridge) | Paul Coates | Pete Norton |
| Tranmere on Tour | Mark White | Becky Brushwood |
| Chronicle & Echo | Ollerton Stags | Crewe Cobbler |
| Gordon McMillan (Cambridge) | Northampton Town Football Club | |

www.ingramcontent.com/pod-product-compliance
Lightning Source LLC
Chambersburg PA
CBHW072051110526
44590CB00018B/3127